Celtic Style
Floral Appliqué

Celtic Style Floral Appliqué

Designs Using Interlaced Scrollwork

by

Scarlett Rose

American Quilter's Society

P. O. Box 3290 • Paducah, KY 42002-3290

ACKNOWLEDGMENTS

Thank you to all the ladies of the Quilter's Sew-ciety of Redding, especially the TNT's (you know who you are!), and also to Kitty Pippen, Sheryl and Yogiro Sadohara, and all those who have encouraged me through the years.

Library of Congress Cataloging-in-Publication Data

Rose, Scarlett.
    Celtic style floral appliqué : designs using interlaced scrollwork
/ by Scarlett Rose.
          p.   cm.
    Includes bibliographical references.
    ISBN 0-89145 -841-7
    1. Appliqué -- Patterns.   2. Decoration and ornament, Celtic.
3. Decoration and ornament -- Plant forms.   4. Quilts.   I. Title.
TT779.R67   1995
746.44'5--dc20   94--46521
                                                                                    CIP

Additional copies of this book may be ordered from:

American Quilter's Society
P.O. Box 3290
Paducah, KY 42002-3290
@14.95. Add $1.00 for postage and handling.

Copyright: 1994, Scarlett Rose

DEDICATION

In memory of my Mother,
Yoko Goto Rose
(1927–1992)

Would that my Mother might live a thousand years
Would there were on this earth no final parting
Ariwara Narihira

Yo no nakani sa ra nu wakare no na ku mo ga na
Chi yo mo to na ge ku hito no ko no ta me
Ariwara Narihira

CREDITS

The following photos were taken by Richard Walker for the American Quilter's Society: Figs. 6-1, 6-5, 6-8, 6-11, 6-14, and 6-17.

The photo of the author was taken by Tom Schmidt of T.A. Schmidt & Associates, Redding, California.

All other photos were taken by Scarlett Rose.

The retranslation of the Japanese poem in the dedication back into the original Japanese was done by Yogiro Sadohara.

CONTENTS

Introduction

Celtic scrollwork was used centuries ago in Ireland to embellish objects of art such as Gospel books and tombstones with graceful interlaced patterns. In Celtic style appliqué, bias strips form the interlaced patterns, with fabric insets between the "knots."

In this book I have added a new design element to the Celtic scrollwork, flowers and leaves, and I have changed the scrollwork into twining stems. I designed nine original blocks, plus border patterns, from which you can make pillows, wallhangings, or full-size quilts. You will find color photos of six Celtic floral appliqué quilts for you to make or to inspire you to try your own ideas.

Think of your first block of Celtic floral appliqué as a practice piece. After you have worked out any problem areas with the technique, I think you will enjoy making these designs and seeing what you can do with them.

I have tried to include enough information so that anyone who would like to make one of my designs will be able to do so. Beginners, though, may wish to consult the books listed in the bibliography for more information on basic appliqué and quiltmaking techniques, or take a class.

This is only the beginning of my exploration of interlaced scrollwork. I have many more designs drawn and plenty of ideas for more variations. This book includes many variations that I have thought of, but haven't made yet. As the saying goes, so many ideas, so little time.

HOW THIS BOOK STARTED

I designed pieced quilts for several years, resisting handwork as being too difficult. But after taking a class in hand appliqué that taught the technique of using basted paper pieces, I decided that technique would work for me. When freezer paper appliqué was introduced, I enthusiastically learned that method as well.

Once I had practiced on a few blocks, I set out to find a style of appliqué that I would enjoy the most. I tried a variety of styles before coming across a book on Celtic appliqué. This was it! I knew I had found the style that I wanted to explore. I made several blocks using the patterns in that book and then started to experiment with drawing my own blocks. I studied a book on how to draw Celtic designs, which helped me to design my own patterns.

As I looked through other art books, there were designs that were similar to Celtic interlace, but which had originated in different cultures. It seemed that the idea of interlaced scrollwork had been done in variations all over the world, as well as in Ireland. The kind done in the Asian countries, Japan in particular, caught my eye. My mother is Japanese, so I have always been interested in Japanese art. I think this is why my designs developed the way they did.

I bought several books with pictures of interlaced designs for inspiration. Using a photocopy machine to enlarge designs that were too small, I played around with the variations created by the different cultures. This gave me a feel for what was possible to do with interlacing. I added the flowers to the scrollwork I had drawn to give the blocks a different look, something more representative of who and what I am.

I started to appliqué some of my new patterns without any real idea of what would become of them. As I worked, the idea gradually emerged that I could make a quilt. When I designed a lattice, I realized at that point that the quilt was actually a traditional American type in many respects. It was going to be a Celtic design sampler quilt, the blocks set with lattices and a border.

I worked on this project for months, carrying the blocks with me to quilt guild meetings. Everyone kept asking me what I was making, and for a long time, I said "I don't know." As the design began to come together, it was exciting to see my sampler quilt emerge. I realized that I hadn't seen any quilts made with patterns like mine and that I was doing something different. I started to think of other ways of using the block designs.

Then the idea of doing a series of wallhangings suggested itself to me. I drew a pattern using one of the block designs for the center and modified the border design. I deliberately chose a different color scheme from the one I had used in my sampler quilt. I also changed some of the design details in the wallhanging to give it individuality. I had hardly started stitching the first one when I started drawing the next design. I was hooked!

At the same time, I started to send my finished sampler quilt, named "Celtic Orchids," to various competitions. It received very good judge's sheets and was a Best of Show winner at a local quilt show. When people started to ask me where I had gotten the pattern for the quilt, I began to think about publishing my designs. It seemed a good idea, but I had no experience at the time in going about it. As I was making the wallhangings, I started researching the process of getting a book published. I also began teaching an appliqué class using my block designs, learning a lot from all my students.

This book is the result of all that work. I am thrilled and excited to share these designs with others.

Basic Supplies

This chapter lists the special tools that you will need to do Celtic floral appliqué. Some of the tools are necessary; some are optional. If you cannot find the tool you need in your local quilt shop, see the Sources section at the end of this book for mail order options.

BIAS BAR *(Fig. 1-1)*. A long, thin piece of metal or plastic, it is used as a pressing aid for the bias strips of fabric which form the interlacing part of the design. Bias bars come in several widths for different sizes of finished strips. The patterns in this book require a ¼" (6mm) bias bar. I prefer metal bars, made of aluminum. The plastic ones I have tried are too thick and have ridges on them. This makes the fabric harder to slide on the bar and doesn't give you a nice sharp crease when you press the strip with the bar inside.

TOPSTITCHING OR EDGESTITCHING FOOT

(Fig. 1-2.) This specialized foot for your sewing machine is used to guide the line of stitching a uniform distance from the edge of the fabric. I use one to help me sew an even seam on the narrow bias strips. Some sewing machines come with this accessory. Other machines can use a generic foot which can be purchased from a sewing machine dealer or mail order source. There is also a specialized foot, called the Fastube™ Sewing Foot, that can be used to sew the bias strips. Of course, you can use a regular clear plastic foot, but if you intend to make many blocks, using one of these specialized feet will make the sewing easier and more accurate.

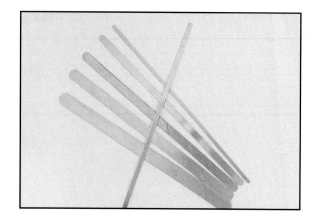

Fig. 1-1. *Bias bars.*

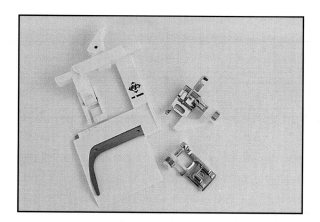

Fig. 1-2. *Topstitching or edgestitching feet.*

HAND APPLIQUÉ NEEDLES. Hand appliqué needles are called sharps. They are long, thin needles that come in a range of sizes – the bigger the number, the smaller the needle. Use the smallest size you feel comfortable with. Small needles are less likely to distort the fabric. Pushing a large needle through the fabric can make a big hole and also cause the appliqué to shift from its proper position. The smaller the needle, the easier it will pass through the fabric with the least effort.

NEEDLE THREADER. I list needle threaders because I have encountered so many people who have problems threading small needles. There are needle threaders available that can be used to thread the smallest size needles without difficulty.

If your vision is not as good as it used to be, here are a few tips which may help. First, make sure your glasses are the correct prescription. Also, there are magnifying lenses available for needleworkers that you might consider. Another helpful hint is to thread several needles onto a spool of thread in the morning when your eyes are rested. When you undo the thread, just push all but one of the needles farther down, cutting off a length of thread to sew with that has just one needle on it. The rest remain on the spool until you have used up the first piece of thread (Fig. 1-3). (This can also be a way to help you schedule a set amount of sewing. Thread four needles on a spool and then make sure you do at least that much sewing for each day. This may help you get a project finished by setting yourself a small daily goal.) Finally, ask someone to thread some needles for you. Some of the quilters I know do this so their grandchildren can be "helpful."

THIMBLE (Fig. 1-4). Use a thimble to protect your finger while appliquéing. For a long time I sewed without one. After making a sore spot on my finger from pushing the needle, I would not sew for a couple of days to let the finger heal. Keep trying different thimbles until you find one you can live with. It is worth the effort to save the wear and tear on your fingers. At last, I found the thimble meant for me, and now I sew all the time without making my fingers sore.

FREEZER PAPER. This paper is used for the method of preparing appliqué pieces described in Chapter 5. Freezer paper has a plastic coating on one side and can be purchased at grocery stores.

DRAWING PAPER. I use large sheets of paper to put together most of my full-size patterns. Check with your local newspaper to see if you can

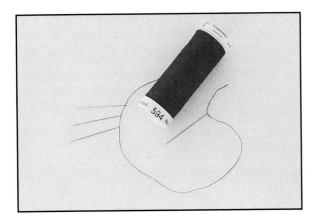

Fig. 1-3. *Threaded needles.*

Fig. 1-4. *Thimbles.*

purchase roll ends of blank newsprint. You can also tape pieces of paper together to get a big enough piece for a whole design.

TRACING PAPER. Transparent paper, such as onion skin or parchment paper, is used for making a copy of the flower design from a block, to serve as a guide for positioning the flower pieces onto the background when you can't see the marks. It can also be used for copying your patterns (see Chapter 3). You can buy tracing paper at office supply stores and art stores.

ROTARY CUTTER, RULER, AND MAT. If you don't have a rotary cutter, you can use a ruler to mark the bias strips and cut them with scissors. Rotary cutters are a truly wonderful invention, but they are expensive to buy since you also need a mat and ruler. It also takes some practice to learn how to use a rotary cutter correctly. I almost threw my first rotary cutter away because I couldn't get it to cut cleanly. As with buying a specialized foot for your sewing machine, getting a rotary cutter set is dependent on whether or not you will be using it enough to justify the purchase. The ruler should be a big one, preferably 6" x 24" (15.2cm x 60.9cm), for cutting the long bias strips. The mat should be at least 18" x 24" (45.7cm x 60.9cm).

MARKING PEN OR PENCIL FOR FABRIC. The marking pen I use most often is a silver pencil. I also use chalk pencils. There are many different types of markers available. Use one you are comfortable with and which gives you visible but removable lines.

SEWING MACHINE IN GOOD WORKING ORDER. Sewing the bias strips is the only part of Celtic floral appliqué for which you will need a sewing machine. For sewing the strips, use a size 12/80 needle, with either a sharp or a universal point. "In good working order" refers to whether the machine has been maintained. When was the last time you changed the needle? When was your sewing machine last cleaned and oiled? I do this routine maintenance myself on my machines on a regular basis. A sewing machine can only work well when it is taken care of properly.

PAPER SCISSORS. Please don't use your good fabric scissors for cutting the freezer paper or paper templates.

FABRIC SCISSORS. Buy the best quality fabric scissors you can afford. It makes so much difference when you have to do a lot of cutting.

PINS. Use small pins to avoid stabbing yourself. Some people use small safety pins. I'm somewhat of an anti-pin person. Only when it is absolutely necessary do I use pins.

LAMP. Having good light to sew by makes all the difference in the world. I use a 100 watt lamp for sewing by hand or machine. This lamp clamps onto my sewing table and is adjustable so that I can shine the light right where I want it. When I do hand sewing in my favorite chair, I have a floor lamp that adjusts so the light falls where I need it. For years I sewed with only room light and wondered why my eyes felt so tired. I finally learned that having good light would save me from a lot of eyestrain and that I could sew more accurately if I could see what I was doing.

IRON. You will need an iron to press the edges of the freezer paper appliqué templates. I strongly recommend a small travel iron rather than the larger types used for ironing clothes. The small iron is easier to handle when working with small pieces of fabric and transfers heat better from the tip and edges than the large irons do. You do not need steam to press the freezer paper.

Fabric Selection

I don't follow any particular color theory in choosing fabrics. Most of what I've learned comes from looking at quilts and studying books. I recommend several books on fabric and color in the bibliography at the end of this book. I've found that there are so many different shades of each color, that if you look long enough, you will find just the right shades to make any combination of colors work. You can follow the color suggestions for the quilts in this book, or you can work on developing a color sense of your own.

You will need to choose fabric for the background, the bias strips, the insets, and the floral appliqué pieces. Keep in mind that the more the interlaced strips contrast with the background, the better the design will show up. Fabrics, especially prints which are similar, will tend to blend in to each other. Large or medium scale prints will probably work better for the insets than for the strips or small flower pieces.

The color pictures in this book show how fabric selection can vary the look of a block. The quilts use the same block designs, but each uses different solid colors, as well as marbled, printed, or lamé fabric. All four of my medallion wallhangings use some of these different types of fabrics to help create a different personality for each. In Celtic Orchids (*Fig. 6-1, page 34*), all the bias strips are solid green. Using different shades of

green or different colors for strips in the same knot can emphasize the interweave effect.

The sample blocks in *Fig. 2-1*, page 14, use primarily calico fabrics. The contrast between them and the blocks in Celtic Orchids is striking because of the different fabric choices. Compare Celtic Orchids Block #3 from the sampler quilt (*Fig. 2-2*, page 14) with the same block made in calico (*Fig. 2-3*, page 14). The first block uses dramatic high contrast solid colors: black, white, green, and burgundy. In the second block the printed fabrics create a softer look, even though some of the same colors are used. The insets in the two blocks are done in different colors and different areas are filled.

When you compare the quilts in this book, also look at the different fabrics used for the insets. This detail alone can really change a block's appearance. You may want to try centering a motif from a large scale print in the insets.

The photos in this book will give you some ideas of the possibilities of what truly different color combinations can do for a design. I try to collect fabric in all colors, even colors I may not like for clothing or furnishings. I find that a little bit of a color that I don't like by itself may be just what is needed to make a quilt sparkle.

For example, Celtic Medallion IV (*Fig. 6-12*, page 57) uses a color scheme that few people

Fig. 2-1. *Sample blocks.*

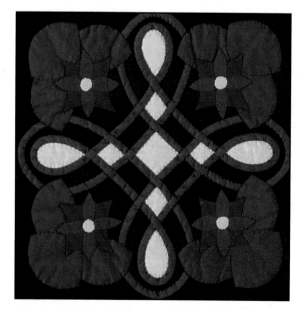

Fig. 2-2. *Block #3 from Celtic Orchids quilt.*

Fig. 2-3. *Block #3 done in calico fabric.*

thought would work. When I say I made a wall-hanging using purple and orange, most people shudder. After they see it, they realize that the shades of the colors make all the difference. The purple is actually periwinkle, just that shade which when placed next to blue looks purple, but when placed next to purple looks blue. I started with the periwinkle fabric for the background and picked the colors for the bias strips, leaves, and flowers. There is yellow, burgundy, and green, as well as pumpkin orange for the flowers.

This was a new combination for me to attempt. I don't like orange and using so much of it in this wallhanging was really a challenge.

If you need to shop for more fabric, tape sample pieces of fabrics you have already chosen to a card (*Fig. 2-4*) so you can try out new fabric combinations in the stores. This is how I collect what I need for several projects at one time. These cards don't take up much room in my purse and are easy to use wherever I am. If you prefer, you can take whole pieces of fabric instead.

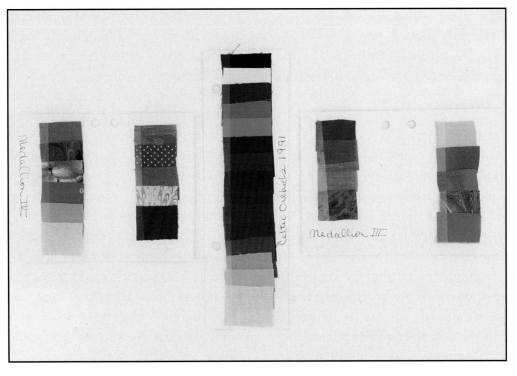

Fig. 2-4. *Fabric card.*

Drawing the Design

All the designs in this book are full-size and do not need to be enlarged. The patterns are drawn in parts which are mostly 6" (15.2cm) squares (some are other sizes). To make the quilts, put the squares together like a puzzle. Each Celtic appliqué block is made of four squares. The quilts are made of the appliqué blocks, plus border and corner blocks and lattices. Look through the pattern diagrams (*Figs. 6-2, 6-5, 6-8, 6-11, and 6-13*) to see how the quilts are put together.

Located in Chapters 8 and 9 are the block patterns, Celtic Orchids Blocks #1 through 9, the border patterns, Sections #1 through 21, and Diagram A, which shows how to place bias strips in the lattices.

COPYING THE PATTERN PIECES

The easiest way to copy the patterns from this book is to photocopy them. If you don't have access to a photocopy machine, use tracing paper to copy the block patterns from the book. I do this a lot when I am working on a design late at night when no businesses are open.

After tracing a design from the book with tracing paper, use a light box or window to copy the pattern onto regular paper. In the daytime, I tape patterns to a large window in my house. My neighbors are accustomed to seeing all kinds of things on my windows! Tape a copy of the pattern to the window with a sheet of paper over it. Then trace the pattern onto this paper. I draw my patterns in pencil first and then go over the lines with a black felt tip pen.

If you use a large enough piece of paper, you can get a whole quilt design on one sheet. I use this method of copying to make most of my full-size quilt patterns. You can also tape pieces of paper together to get a big enough piece for a whole design. If you don't have large sheets of paper, an alternative method is to trace or photocopy each section of the design from the book, trim with scissors and then tape them together to get a full-size quilt pattern.

Either process of making a full-size pattern allows you an opportunity to make changes in the design. Some of my best ideas came from a mistake in tracing. I don't admit to making any errors; I call them "design decisions."

PUTTING THE PATTERN PIECES TOGETHER

The Celtic Orchid blocks are each made up of four squares arranged in a 2 x 2 grid. To make the pattern for a complete block, trace or photocopy the pattern in the book four times. Some of the blocks have two patterns, one the reverse of the other. For these blocks, make two copies of each square and arrange in a 2 x 2 grid.

I will use Celtic Medallion II as an example of

preparing a pattern for a medallion quilt. First draw a 36" (91.2cm) square on a large piece of paper. Grid the paper so it is entirely made up of 6" (15.2cm) squares (*Fig. 3-1*). Starting from the outside of the quilt, working in toward the center, you will trace sections and blocks into the grid squares. (If you have made photocopies, tape or glue the copies to the grid instead of tracing.)

Check the layout diagram of the quilt (*Fig. 3-2*, page 18) for the orientation of each block. Some of the sections will need to be rotated so that the bias strips line up properly to form the knot designs. *Fig. 3-2* shows which sections go in which grid squares.

To make the pattern for Celtic Medallion II, first place Section #9 in each of the corners with the loops pointing outward. Next to the corners are Section #2 blocks. As you can see, the unfinished knot in Section #9 matches Section #2, which is actually half of a 6" x 12" (15.2cm x 30.4cm) knot. In the middle of this border place a complete Section #2 knot (two Section #2 blocks, oriented left and right). Place two flowers from Celtic Orchids Block #8 on each edge of this outer border, joining the loops formed by the Section #2 blocks. The flower centers should be 2¼" (57mm) from the inside edge of this border. Check the layout diagram or photo (*Fig. 6-7*, page 46) for the correct rotation of the flowers.

Divide the next row of the 6" (15.2cm) grid into 3" (7.6cm) strips (lattices) all the way around. Center Section #11 in each of the outermost 3" (7.6cm) strips, with 10½" (26.65cm) on either side. The innermost 3" (7.6cm) lattice has bias strips on each edge. See Diagram A, page 125, and the photo of the quilt for placing these bias strips. Place Section #10 in each corner of this lattice with the loops pointing outward.

Place Celtic Orchids Block #8 in the center four squares of the grid.

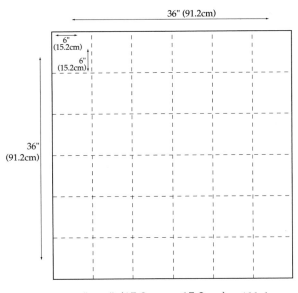

Fig. 3-1. 6" x 6" (15.2cm x 15.2cm) *gridded paper for preparing the Medallion Quilt patterns.*

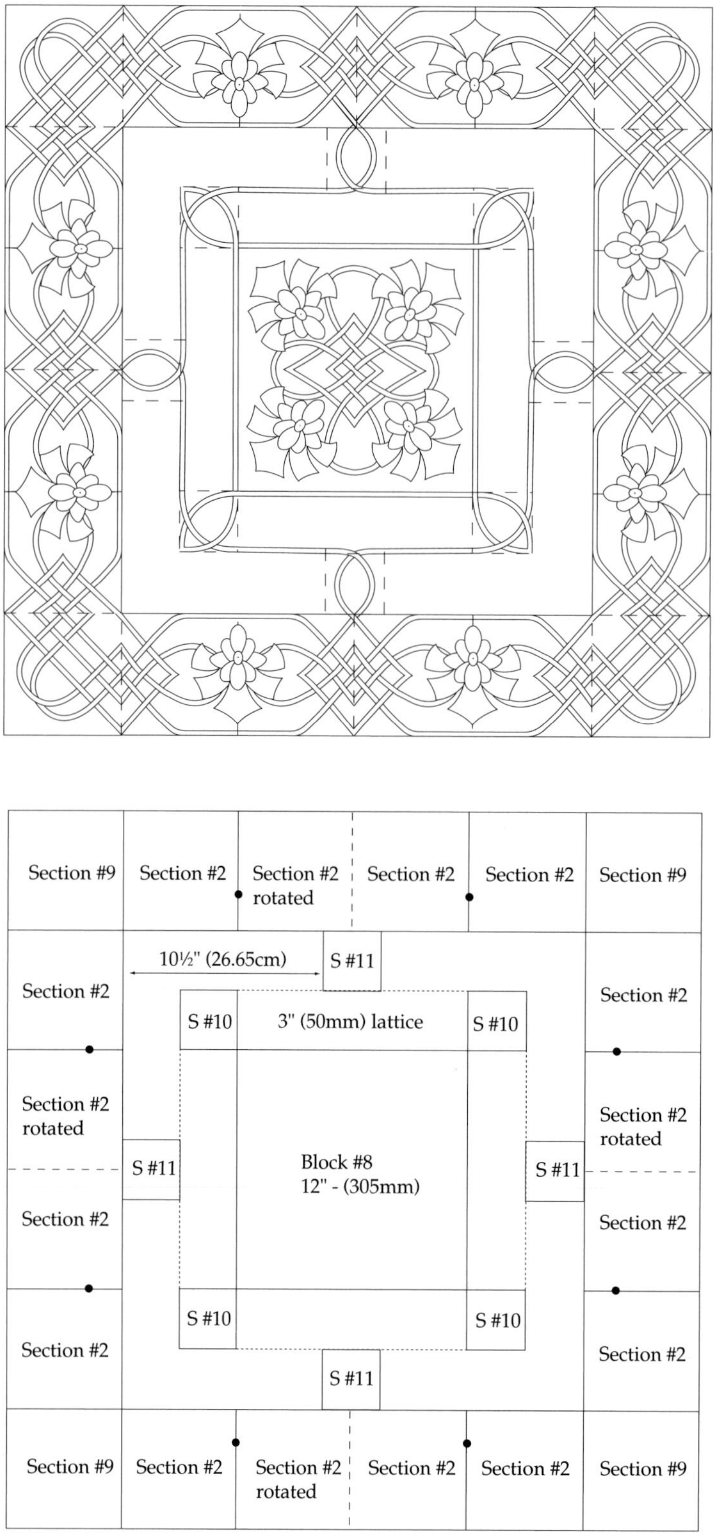
Section #9
Section #2
Section #2 rotated
Section #2
Section #2
Section #9
Section #2
10½" (26.65cm)
S #11
Section #2
S #10
3" (50mm) lattice
S #10
Section #2 rotated
Section #2 rotated
S #11
Block #8
12" - (305mm)
S #11
Section #2
Section #2
S #10
S #10
Section #2
Section #2
S #11
Section #9
Section #2
Section #2 rotated
Section #2
Section #2
Section #9

Fig. 3-2. *Celtic Medallion II, Layout Diagram.*

TRANSFERRING THE PATTERN ONTO THE BACKGROUND FABRIC

After drawing the full-size copy of the quilt on paper, you are ready to trace the design onto the background fabric. If the fabric is light colored, you may be able to see the design through the fabric. (That's why I mark the lines on the paper with a black felt pen – to give a good, dark line that I can see through a variety of fabrics.) If you cannot see the pattern through the background fabric, you will need to use a large window or a light box.

I usually cut the background fabric several inches larger than the finished size. "Finished size" means the size of the completed quilt (Celtic Medallion II is 40" x 40" or approx. 1m x 1m), **not** the size of the gridded paper pattern.

To transfer the pattern to the background fabric, tape the paper pattern on a flat surface, such as a window, table, or the floor. Then tape the fabric on top of the copy, centering it so there is the same amount of fabric on all sides. Trace the design onto the fabric using your fabric marking pen or pencil. Make sure that you have traced all of the parts of the design. One way to check for this is to slide a piece of white paper between the fabric and the drawing so any blank areas will show up.

Sewing Instructions

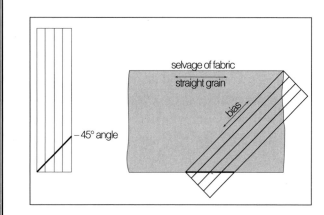

Fig. 4-1a. *Use a ruler with a 45° angle marked on it.*

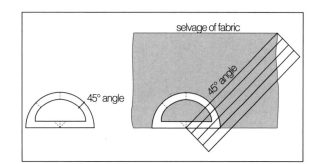

Fig. 4-1b. *Use a protractor.*

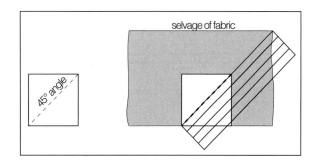

Fig. 4-1c. *Use a right triangle made from a square of paper, fold corner to corner diagonally.*

After you have drawn your pattern onto the background fabric (see Chapter 3), you are ready to sew. These instructions will explain the steps of preparing and sewing the bias strips, the insets, and the floral appliqué.

Cutting the Bias Strips

For the ¼" (6mm) finished size bias strips used in these patterns, you need to cut strips of bias fabric ⅞" (23mm) wide. Don't seam these together – you'll be hiding the ends so that you won't need really long pieces. If you are sewing one block, cut four bias strips from ¼ yard (23cm) of fabric.

Figs. 4-1a – c show three ways to cut bias strips. The easiest way to cut the strips is with a ruler marked with a 45 degree angle. Line up the mark with the selvage of the fabric and cut the strips using a rotary cutter, or mark lines on the fabric and cut with scissors. If you don't have a ruler that has this marked line, use a protractor to give you the correct angle. If you don't have a protractor, take a piece of paper, mark and cut a perfect square. Fold the square on the diagonal from one corner to another. This diagonal will be your guide for a 45 degree angle.

Cutting ⅞" (23mm) strips will allow you slightly more than ⅛" (3mm) for the seam allowances. Fold the strips in half with the **right** side of the fabric out *(Fig. 4-2)*.

SEWING THE BIAS STRIPS

After sewing miles of strips with such a small seam allowance, I realized that it is much easier to use the *folded* edge as my guide instead of the cut edge *(Fig. 4-3)*. I set my edgestitching foot to slightly larger than ¼" (6mm) and then sew the strip with the fold up against the guide of the foot. I have found that this way my sewing machine has better traction on the fabric since more of the strip is under the foot. Your sewing may be a little wavy on your first bias strip, but it will get better quickly with practice.

Use a stitch length of about 12 to 14 stitches to the inch (25mm). Feed the strips through the sewing machine one after another and then clip them apart. I sew batches of twelve or so at a time, and then press and appliqué those before making more. For a large project like Celtic Orchids you will need to make lots of strips. I find that breaking the sewing up into smaller groups of strips isn't so overwhelming as trying to sew up a whole quilt's worth at one time.

PRESSING THE BIAS STRIPS

Next, slide a ¼" (6mm) bias bar inside a sewn strip and roll the seam allowance over so that it can be pressed flat on one side and not be visible on the other *(Fig. 4-4)*. Press the strip with the bar inside. Move the bar down the strip if the strip is longer than the bar. The aluminum can get hot, so don't press all the way along the bar. Leave a little space at one end untouched so you can pick up the bar and wave it in the air for a second to cool it off. (Plastic bars don't have this problem, so if you can find thin, smooth ones, they would be an improvement on the metal ones.) Press the strip again after removing the bias bar so you will have a nice flat strip.

Fig. 4-3. *Sewing the bias strip.*

Fig. 4-2. *Folded bias strip.*

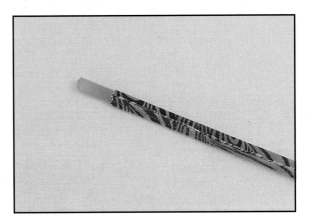

Fig. 4-4. *Pressed bias strip on bias bar.*

PREPARING THE INSETS

The next step is to prepare the fabric insets which will fill some spaces within the bias scrollwork. If you study the photos in this book, you will see that you can be creative in your choice of inset shapes and placement.

Using the block pattern, trace any areas where you want to put an inset. Don't forget seam allowances. The seam allowances should be a generous ⅛" (3mm), enough to allow the bias strips to anchor the inset in place, but not so much that the raw edges show beyond the bias strips. If you wish to use a large inset that will cover an area where strips pass across it, trace the needed lines onto the inset.

Baste the insets to the background fabric *(Fig. 4-5)*.

APPLIQUÉING AND INTERWEAVING THE BIAS STRIPS

When I appliqué the bias strips, I do not use pins. I place a strip on the marked lines of the background fabric, curving the strip along the lines as I sew it *(Fig. 4-6)*. I sew one strip at a time. If you prefer, you can baste the strips and then sew them. However, with this method there is the risk of misjudging the length of strips and having to stretch or ease them to fit the design, resulting in a distorted block that won't lie flat.

To sew the appliqué stitch, knot the end of your thread and insert your threaded needle from underneath the background fabric up through the edge of the strip and pull the thread through. Then insert the needle down into the fabric near where the thread came out, and up through the background fabric and edge of the strip about ⅛" (3mm) or less from the first stitch *(Fig. 4-7a & b, page 23)*. Sew one stitch at a time. With practice, your appliqué stitches will be small and even, with the appliquéd piece lying flat with no puckers or stretching.

I usually start with a strip that comes out from a flower. It doesn't really matter which one you start with, though. Start the strip a little ways under the flower to make sure the flower pieces can cover the end of the strip without raw edges showing. If the strip curves or turns a corner, stitch the inside edge first.

As you come to an intersection of strips, check the pattern to see if the strip you are sewing passes under or over the intersecting

Fig. 4-5. *Inset basted onto the background fabric.*

Fig. 4-6. *Sewing the first bias strip.*

strip. If it passes under *(Fig. 4-8)*, you can keep on sewing. If it passes over *(Fig. 4-9)*, you need to leave a big enough opening so the intersecting strip can fit through. I usually take a really big stitch, leaving enough space between two stitches for the opening. I use a stiletto or a pin to push a strip through an opening.

The strips interweave, forming a two dimensional knot. (If you were to twist a piece of string into the shape of the design and pull on the ends, it would make a true three dimensional knot.) The rhythm of under and over repeats as you appliqué along each strip. There are never two unders or two overs next to each other.

Double check the pattern as you come to intersections to help prevent mistakes. If it is a problem to remember to leave openings at every other intersection, you can leave openings at every intersection. It took me a couple of blocks to get into the rhythm of under and over, and I still make mistakes now and then. If you make a mistake, carefully pick out the stitches in the spot where you need an opening. When you are sewing along the strip that passes through this opening, take a couple of stitches on either side to anchor the top strip down.

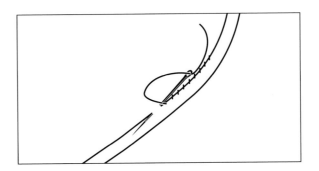

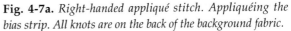

Fig. 4-7a. *Right-handed appliqué stitch. Appliquéing the bias strip. All knots are on the back of the background fabric.*

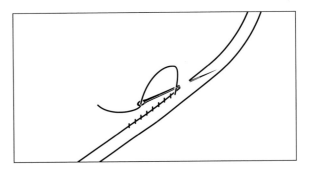

Fig. 4-7b. *Left-handed appliqué stitch. Appliquéing the bias strip. All knots are on the back of the background fabric.*

Fig. 4-8. *Strip which crosses underneath.*

Fig. 4-9. *Strip which crosses over.*

It isn't necessary to use a strip long enough to reach from one flower to another. A strip can end at an intersection where it passes underneath another strip. Sew a few stitches to secure the end of the strip to the background fabric. Place the beginning of the next strip against the end of the first strip, secure with a few stitches and continue the design *(Fig. 4-10)*. The strip that crosses over an intersection where two ends are butted up against each other will hide the ends. No one will know that the ends are there when the block is finished. This way, you can use short strips *(Fig. 4-11)*.

When you come to a corner in the design, stitch right up to the inside angle and take an extra stitch there. Then fold the strip back on itself with the fold edge even with the outside marked line *(Fig. 4-12)*. Press firmly with your finger. Using your needle on the outside corner to hold the strip in place, turn the strip right side up and line it up with the marked line as it continues after the corner. This forms a miter in the corner *(Fig. 4-13)*. When you are stitching back along the other side of the strip, be sure to place a couple of stitches along this diagonal line to keep the excess from popping out. If the corner looks like it will

Fig. 4-10. *Butted ends will be hidden by the strip crossing over.*

Fig. 4-11. *Using short strips.*

Fig. 4-12. *Folding the bias strip to make a corner.*

Fig. 4-13. *Sewing the mitered corner.*

be too bulky, carefully trim the seam allowance of the strip before you sew the miter. When the mitered point is a long sharp one, also trim a little of the excess strip itself. Be careful not to cut too much, as it is easier to trim more if the first cut doesn't remove enough, but if too much is cut, you will have to replace the strip.

PREPARING THE FLORAL APPLIQUÉ PIECES

After stitching all the bias strips, it is time to start on the leaves and flowers. After trying a lot of different methods of appliqué, I have found that the freezer paper and paper basting methods work the best in giving me the results I want. Stitching is more relaxing to me if I don't have to struggle with turning under the seam allowances as I sew.

FREEZER PAPER METHOD. With this method I press the seam allowances of the fabric around the edges of a freezer paper template. The freezer paper, when heated, works like a temporary adhesive. This gives you an exact piece, all ready to be stitched down on the background fabric.

PAPER BASTING METHOD. Before learning of the freezer paper method, I hand basted the seam allowances around a plain paper template.

To prepare the pieces for appliqué, first trace the leaves and flowers onto freezer paper or regular paper, depending on the appliqué method you choose. Make sure to number both sides of the pieces. These numbers indicate the order in which the pieces need to be appliquéd. Pin the pieces to the wrong side of the fabric and cut them out, adding a ¼" (6mm) seam allowance. (If you are experienced with this method, you may be able to use smaller seam allowances.) If you are using freezer paper, be sure that the shiny side is away from the wrong side of the fabric, so when the seam allowances are pressed over the

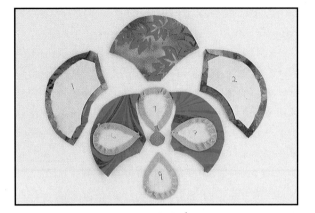

Fig. 4-14. *Appliqué pieces prepared with freezer paper templates.*

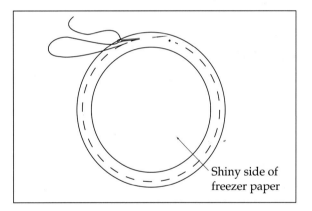

Fig. 4-15a. *Preparing circular appliqué pieces. Sew a basting stitch in the seam allowance and pull the thread to cause the seam allowance to curl around the template.*

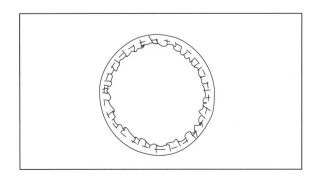

Fig. 4-15b. *Press with an iron and then remove the basting stitches.*

paper they stick to the shiny side *(Fig. 4-14, page 25)*.

Roll the seam allowance over, feeling the edge of the template, and carefully press a smooth edge with the tip or edge of the iron. This skill improves quickly with practice. If the edge is not completely smooth, peel up the seam allowance and repress it.

To press a small circle or oval I first baste the edges to the template, like a yo-yo *(Figs. 4-15a & b, page 25)*. This makes pressing such a small piece easier. Then remove the basting thread. I usually use ovals for the flower centers since they are easier to do. If they come out looking egg-shaped when I appliqué them, who's to know I didn't intend them to be that way. Circles will look wrong if they are not perfectly round, and take practice to achieve.

You will note that in the next few figures, there are separate drawings for left-handed and right-handed appliqué. Follow the ones appropri-

ate for you. This method makes it easier to sew the points, which is explained later.

When pressing an inside curve, it is necessary to make small cuts into the seam allowance so that it can fold over the template *(Figs. 4-16a & b)*. Don't notch the seam allowance until just before you press it.

When pressing outside curves, such as the edge of a circle, it is normal for the seam allowances to look ruffled. It is not necessary to notch these curves.

Figs. 4-17a and *4-17b,* page 27, show how to press the points on appliqué pieces. First press one side. Then press the other side, leaving the excess fabric at the point sticking out. It will be taken care of when you appliqué.

Look at the flower pieces carefully and notice that the seam allowances on the edges of some pieces are not turned under. This is because other pieces will lap over them and cover the raw edges. The layering of pieces is why it is so impor-

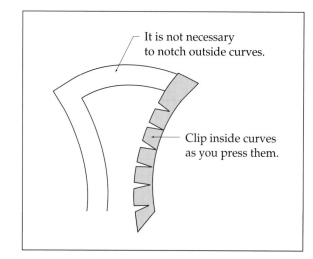

Fig. 4-16a. *Right-handed appliqué. Preparing curved appliqué pieces.*

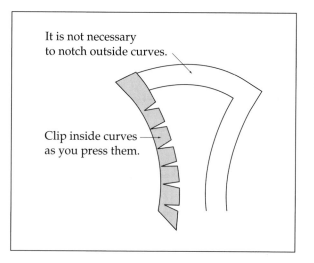

Fig. 4-16b. *Left-handed appliqué. Preparing curved appliqué pieces.*

tant for the pieces to be sewn in the correct order. Check each piece against the pattern to make sure you are cutting it out correctly. The pieces are not reversible and it is easy to cut them out wrong. The flowers are appliquéd one petal at a time, in layers, so they will look like real flowers.

POSITIONING THE FLORAL APPLIQUÉ PIECES

To help you visualize how a flower will look, you may want to lay the pieces on your block pat-tern before sewing them. This gives you a chance to change any of the fabrics you have chosen.

When you are ready to appliqué the pieces, you can use a tracing paper copy of the flower to guide the placement of the pieces if the markings on the background fabric are worn off or covered up (*Fig. 4-18*, page 28). Lay the traced copy on top of the background, lining up the bias strip marks to place it correctly. Then slide each appliqué piece underneath the paper and pin in the proper place.

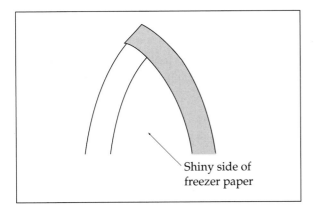

Fig. 4-17a. *Right-handed appliqué. Pressing points on appliqué pieces. Press seam allowance on right side over first.*

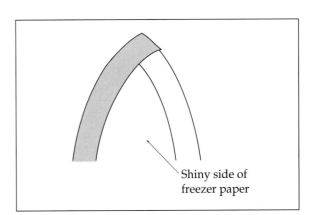

Fig. 4-17b. *Left-handed appliqué. Pressing points on appliqué pieces. Press seam allowance on left side over first.*

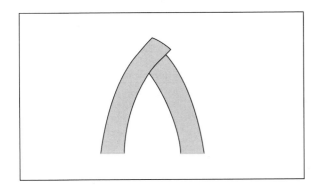

Fig. 4-17ab. *Right-handed appliqué. Press the other seam allowance over. Leave the excess fabric at the point (it will be taken care of when you appliqué).*

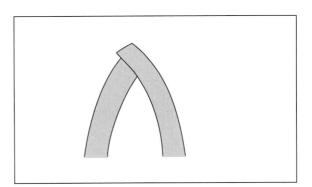

Fig. 4-17bb. *Left-handed appliqué. Press the other seam allowance over. Leave the excess fabric at the point (it will be taken care of when you appliqué).*

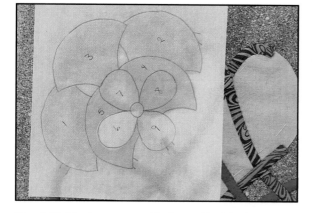

Fig. 4-18. *Tracing paper guide for positioning the appliqué pieces.*

APPLIQUÉING THE FLORAL APPLIQUÉ PIECES

Carefully stitch the prepared pieces to the background in the order that they are numbered. To sew the appliqué stitch, follow the instructions for appliquéing the bias strips. Remember that the goal is to have small stitches, with the appliquéd piece lying flat.

Feel the edge of the template as you sew. If you are sewing through the paper, you are making your stitches too far in. Try sewing closer to the edge of the appliqué piece. If the edge of the piece has small bumps, you can smooth these out by poking them in with your needle before stitching them down. (After some practice, you will be able to press these edges more smoothly and will not need to deal with them when you appliqué.)

When sewing points on appliqué pieces (*Figs. 4-19a & b*), stitch along the piece up to the point. Take an extra stitch in the point. Then trim the excess fabric sticking out to ⅛" (3mm), tuck it under with your needle and continue appliquéing down the next side.

Before sewing all the way around the petal or leaf, remove the freezer paper template with your

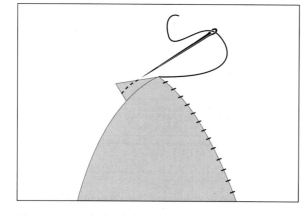

Fig. 4-19a. *Right-handed appliqué. Trim excess fabric to ⅛" (3mm) and tuck under with your needle. Stitch along the right side of the prepared piece. Take an extra stitch in the point.*

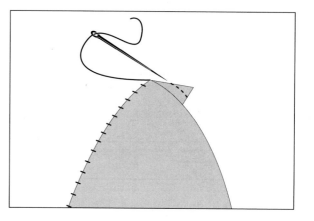

Fig. 4-19b. *Left-handed appliqué. Trim excess fabric to ⅛" (3mm) and tuck under with your needle. Stitch along the left side of the prepared piece. Take an extra stitch in the point.*

fingers or tweezers. If you are using the paper basting method, remove the basting thread and then remove the paper template. Remember to remove each paper template before sewing the next piece. I usually reuse my templates several times.

It is not necessary to cut away the background fabric from the back of the appliqué piece unless you are planning to quilt through that piece. Remove the basting holding the inset pieces.

Figs. 4-20 and *4-21* show the correctly placed appliqué pieces and the finished block.

Fig. 4-20. *Correctly placed appliqué pieces.*

Fig. 4-21. *Finished Celtic Orchids Block #7.*

Finishing Touches

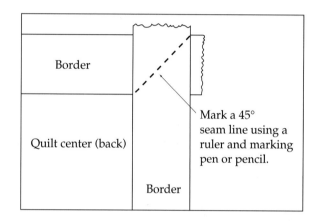

Fig. 5-1a. *Mitering the border corners.*

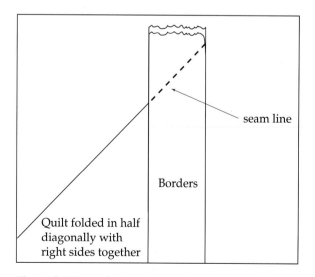

Fig. 5-1b. *Line up border pieces and sew along marked seam line. Trim excess border fabric, leaving ¼" seam. Press to one side.*

COMPLETING THE QUILT TOP

After the top is finished, trim the edges down to the finished size plus ¼" (6mm) seam allowances for sewing on the binding, making the sides straight and the corners square. If the quilt has rounded corners, mark the curves (I use a coffee cup) and cut them.

The Celtic Orchids quilt has a fabric border added after the blocks and lattices are pieced together. *Figs. 5-1a & b* shows how to miter the corners of a border. Cut the border strips to the proper width and center the first two strips on adjacent edges of the quilt. Sew each strip to the edge of the quilt, stopping ¼" (6mm) from the corners. Using a ruler marked with a 45 degree angle, draw a 45 degree seam line on the wrong side of one of the border pieces, extending from the corner outward. Fold the quilt in half on the diagonal with the right sides together. Line up the border strips and sew them together along the marked seam line. Trim off the excess border fabric, leaving a ¼" (6mm) seam. Press the seam to one side. Continue around the quilt, mitering the other three corners.

QUILTING

The instructions for each quilt in Chapter 6 give suggestions for quilting. Quilting can be done outlining the appliquéd design, in straight lines or a grid, or in a design which can be drawn freehand or from a quilting stencil. I've listed some books in the bibliography on quilting and on drafting feather designs. There are also many good classes on quilting.

BINDING THE EDGES OF THE QUILT

See *Figs. 5-2 a – c.* Cut 2½" (64mm) wide bias strips. Sew the strips together into one long piece, mitering the seams. The instructions for each quilt give the length of bias strip needed. Press the strip, with the right side out, in half lengthwise. Sew the folded strip to the front of the quilt along the edges, matching all raw edges. If the corners are square, miter them as follows. Stitch along an edge of the quilt up to ¼" (6mm) from the corner. Make a ½" (12mm) tuck in the binding and start sewing from the same point along the next edge. Miter all four corners, and miter the ends together. Then turn the binding to the back of the quilt, tuck under the raw edges, and hand sew the binding down to finish.

MAKING A SLEEVE

Sew a sleeve onto the back of your finished quilt if you want to hang it on a wall *(Fig. 5-3, page 32)*. A sleeve is essentially a fabric tube. Cut a strip of the backing fabric 10" (25.4cm) wide and slightly shorter than the top edge of the quilt. Hem both ends of the strip. Fold the strip, with the right side out, in half lengthwise and press. Place the strip on the back of the quilt with the folded edge along the top edge of the quilt. Open the strip and baste it to the quilt about 1" (2.54cm) from the fold, making sure your stitches don't go through to the front of the quilt. Then fold the strip back in half, turn both raw edges under ¼" (6mm), and appliqué them to the back of the quilt, making sure your stitches don't go through

Fig. 5-2a. *Piece bias strips to make the full length of binding.*

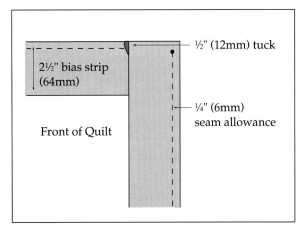

Fig. 5-2b. *Binding the quilt. Stitch the folded binding along one side of the quilt. Stop ¼" (6mm) from the corner. Leaving a ½" (12mm) tuck on the corner, start sewing ¼" (6mm) from the top.*

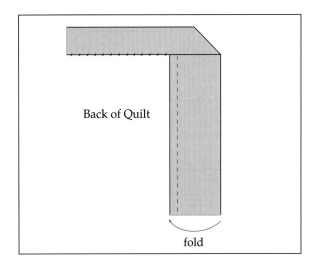

Fig. 5-2c. *Fold the binding to the back, encasing the raw edges. A miter should form on the front at the corner where the tuck is. Fold the remainder of the binding to form another miter on the back.*

to the front of the quilt. The ample space in the sleeve allows room for a round rod, PVC pipe, or wooden stick for hanging the quilt.

SIGNING YOUR QUILT

Be sure to sign the back of the quilt with your name and the date finished. If you wish, include your hometown and country for historical information. Use an indelible ink pen so the writing will be permanent. If the writing won't show on the fabric on the back of the quilt, make a label from a piece of solid color fabric and appliqué it onto the back.

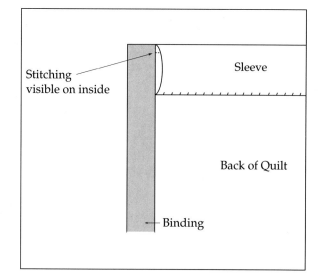

Fig. 5-3. *Making a sleeve for hanging the quilt.*

The Quilts

The Celtic Orchids quilt is a sampler quilt made of nine different Celtic floral appliqué blocks, plus lattices and borders. The other quilts shown in this book are wallhangings. The wallhangings are similar in that each is in the Medallion style with a Celtic Orchids block in the center and a Celtic style border. They are progressive in design: the first set on point, the second set square, the third in a circle, and the fourth in a diamond.

Each wallhanging has its own "look" that I carefully created. I chose the colors to give them their own individuality. Celtic Orchids uses only solid colors, but in the wallhangings I added some hand-marbled fabrics and lamé for sparkle.

For each quilt, I list the materials needed, the block and border patterns used, instructions, and suggestions for quilting and variations. When making one of these quilts, refer to the color photo and the layout diagram. I have included suggested variations for each quilt, plus there are more variations at the end of the chapter which you may want to try.

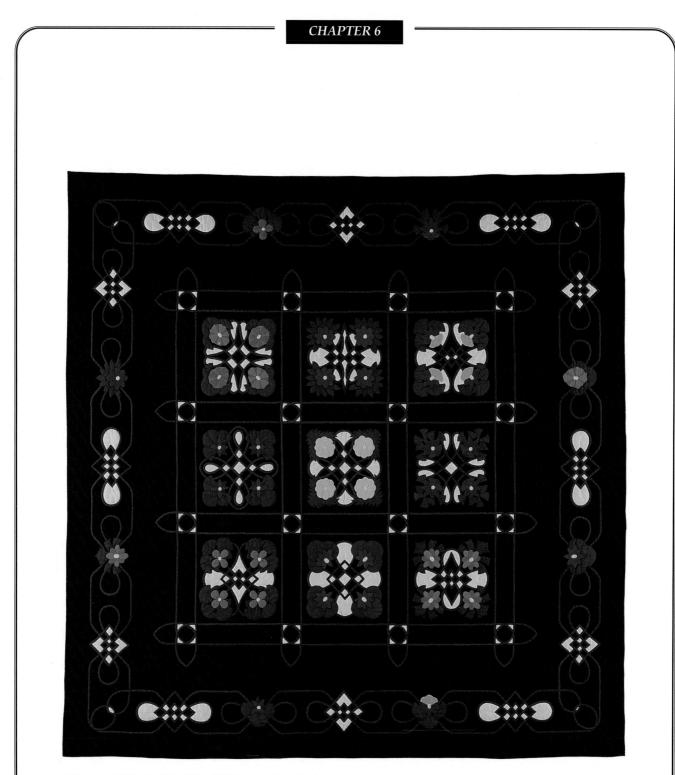

Fig. 6-1. *Celtic Orchids. 78" x 78" (approx. 2m x 2m).*

Celtic Orchids

Finished Size 78" x 78" (approx. 2m x 2m)
See *Figs. 6-1, 6-2, 6-2b, and 6-3*

MATERIALS NEEDED:
   Fabric (44" or 1.14m wide):
   3 yards (2.75m) of solid green for stems and leaves
   6½ yards (6m) of solid black for background and binding
   6¾ yards (6.5m) for backing and hanging sleeve
   ½ yard (45.7cm) of solid white for insets
   ⅛ yard (11.4cm) of each of the following solid colors for flowers:
      light yellow
      medium yellow
      light burgundy
      medium burgundy
      dark burgundy
      light orange
      medium orange
      dark orange
      medium teal
      dark teal
      medium purple
      dark purple
   Matching thread in all colors for appliqué
   Green quilting thread
   ¼" (6mm) bias bar

PATTERNS NEEDED:
   Blocks #1–9,
   Sections #1–6,
   Diagram A for 3" (76mm) lattice.

INSTRUCTIONS:

See *Figs. 6-2a & 6-2b* for placement of blocks and sections. To save time, instead of drawing a separate pattern for each border section, you may wish to draw a full-size pattern of one side of the border to use for tracing the design onto the background fabric. Note that there are different flowers placed along all four sides of the border. Use the color photo as a guide.

The piecing diagram *(Fig. 6-3, page 39)* shows how to put the top together. Add seam allowances to the measurements given. Appliqué the blocks and then sew them together with the lattice pieces. The bias strips for the lattice are sewn on the inner edges (Diagram A, page 125). Appliqué the sides of the border and then attach them to the center portion of the quilt. Appliqué the corner sections last, after mitering the corners *(Figs. 5-1a & b, page 30)*.

QUILTING:

Outline all the appliqué pieces and strips with quilting. Quilt the border in parallel lines 2" (5cm) apart. The quilting lines form a right angle where they meet in the corner.

BINDING:

Make a 2½" (64mm) bias strip for the binding 320" (845cm) long. Sew the binding to the quilt, mitering the corners.

VARIATIONS:

- Use the same knot, but nine different flowers. Center each flower in the space where the original block's flower is and adjust the bias strip lines to fit.
- Use nine different knots, but the same flower. Center the chosen flower where the original block's flowers are and adjust the bias strip lines to fit.
- Appliqué only the knots, omitting all the flowers. Sketch in the missing loops of the bias strips using loops from the blocks or the border as a guideline.
- Appliqué only the flowers. Quilt or trapunto the design of the knots and the bias strips.
- Vary where you put insets, particularly if making the quilt with all the same knot.
- Use different colors for each of the flowers in one block and/or different colors of bias strips.
- Substitute Section #16 – flower corner for Section #1 – corner of border and place a flower in the corner.

Fig. 6-2a. *Celtic Orchids Layout Diagram.*

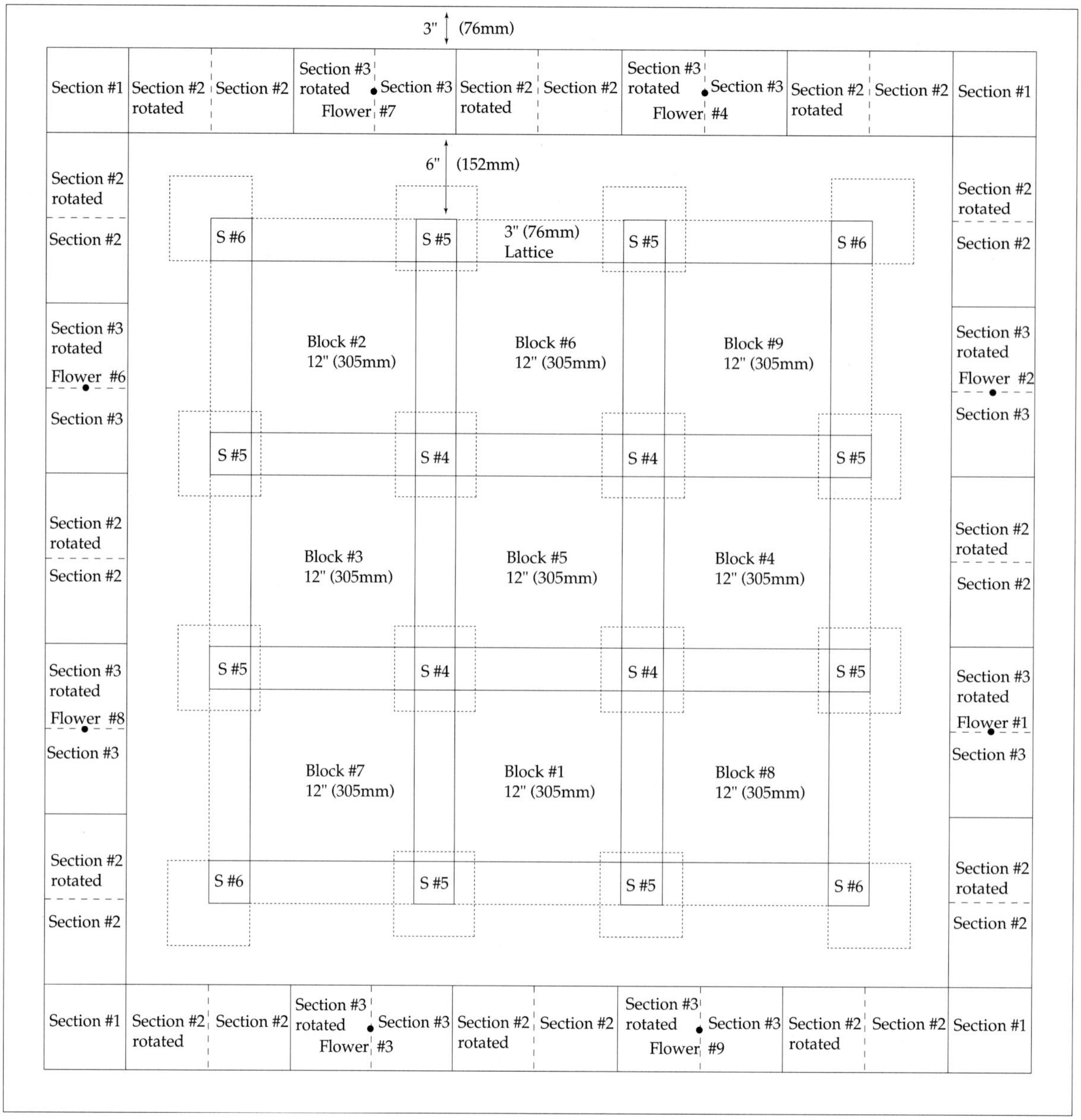

3" (76mm)

| Section #1 | Section #2 rotated | Section #2 | Section #3 rotated Flower #7 | Section #3 | Section #2 rotated | Section #2 | Section #3 rotated Flower #4 | Section #3 | Section #2 rotated | Section #2 | Section #1 |

6" (152mm)

| Section #2 rotated | | | | | | | | Section #2 rotated |
| Section #2 | S #6 | | S #5 | 3" (76mm) Lattice | S #5 | | S #6 | Section #2 |

| Section #3 rotated Flower #6 | | Block #2 12" (305mm) | | Block #6 12" (305mm) | | Block #9 12" (305mm) | | Section #3 rotated Flower #2 |
| Section #3 | | | | | | | | Section #3 |

| | S #5 | | S #4 | | S #4 | | S #5 | |

| Section #2 rotated | | Block #3 12" (305mm) | | Block #5 12" (305mm) | | Block #4 12" (305mm) | | Section #2 rotated |
| Section #2 | | | | | | | | Section #2 |

| Section #3 rotated Flower #8 | S #5 | | S #4 | | S #4 | | S #5 | Section #3 rotated Flower #1 |
| Section #3 | | Block #7 12" (305mm) | | Block #1 12" (305mm) | | Block #8 12" (305mm) | | Section #3 |

| Section #2 rotated | S #6 | | S #5 | | S #5 | | S #6 | Section #2 rotated |
| Section #2 | | | | | | | | Section #2 |

| Section #1 | Section #2 rotated | Section #2 | Section #3 rotated Flower #3 | Section #3 | Section #2 rotated | Section #2 | Section #3 rotated Flower #9 | Section #3 | Section #2 rotated | Section #2 | Section #1 |

Fig. 6-2b. *Celtic Orchids Layout Diagram.*

Section #1 – Corner of border – 6" sq. (152mm)

Section #2 – Border knot – 6" x 12" (152mm x 305mm)

Section #3 – Border knot with flower – 6" x 12" (152mm x 305mm). Each flower is different.

Section #4 – Intersection knot – 3" sq. (76mm)

Section #5 – Edge knot – 3" sq. (76mm)

Section #6 – Corner knot – 3" sq. (76mm)

Blocks #1 – #9 – 12" sq. (305mm)

Lattice strip – 3" x 12" (76mm x 305mm) see Diagram A, page 125.

• – Dots indicate where flowers from Blocks #1, 2, 3, 4, 6, 7, 8, 9 are placed, each has a flower number next to dot. Dot is 2¼" (57mm) from inside edge of border.

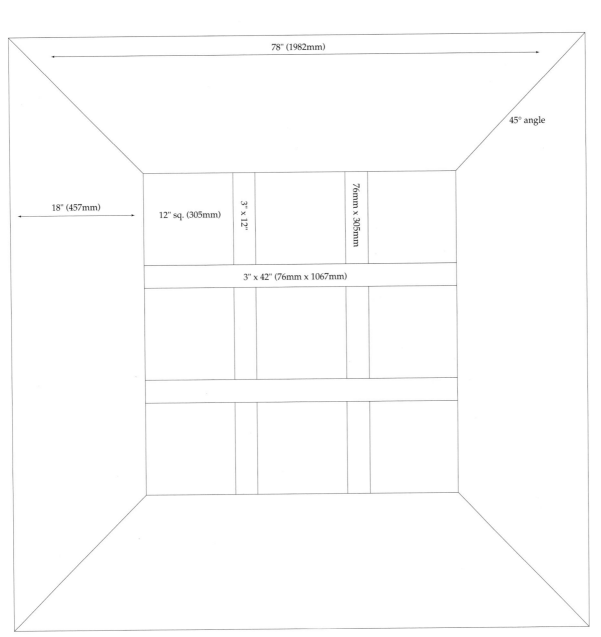

Fig. 6-3. *Celtic Orchids Piecing Diagram, for background fabric and lattices.*

Fig. 6-4. *Celtic Medallion I. 40" x 40" (approx. 1m x 1m)*

Celtic Medallion I

Finished size 40" x 40" (approx. 1m x 1m)
See *Figs. 6-4, 6-5a & b, and 6-6*

MATERIALS NEEDED:
    Fabric (44" or 1.14m wide):
    1¾ yards (1.6m) of solid yellow for background and binding
    ½ yard (46cm) for bias strips and flowers:
        solid light green
        solid medium green
        solid dark green
        marbled green
    ¼ yard (23cm) of gold tricot lamé for insets
    1½ yards (1.4m) for backing and hanging sleeve
    ¼ yard (23cm) of the following for flowers:
        solid lavender
        solid light purple
        solid dark purple
        purple tricot lamé
        marbled purple
    Thread to match all colors for the appliqués
    Yellow quilting thread
    ¼" (6mm) bias bar

PATTERNS NEEDED:
    Block #9
    Sections #1, 2, 7, and 8
    Diagram A for 2" (50mm) lattice.

INSTRUCTIONS:

Draw out a full-size pattern, using *Fig. 6-5a & b* for placement of the sections and block. Trace the design onto a square of background fabric, using the full width of the fabric. Then make the bias strips and prepare the flower and inset pieces. Notice that there are four different greens used for the bias strips and three different colorations of the flowers and leaves. Using the photo as a guide, baste on the insets and appliqué the bias strips and flowers. After trimming the quilt top to the proper size, cut rounded corners.

QUILTING:

Outline all the appliqué pieces and strips with quilting. I added straight lines of quilting wherever I thought they would look good, using a ruler and a marking pencil. You could use any quilting designs that you might have.

BINDING:

Make a 2½" (64mm) bias strip for the binding 170" (432cm) long.

VARIATIONS:
- Use a different block pattern.
- Appliqué the bias strips only, omitting the flowers.
- Appliqué the flowers only, substituting the bias strips with quilting or trapunto. (Fig. 6-6, page 45).
- Change the placement of the insets, use more colors of insets or omit the insets.
- Use one color for all the bias strips.
- Color all the flowers the same.
- Use flowers from other blocks.
- Eliminate some of the flowers, such as the four dark ones on the sides.
- Rotate flowers in the border to face in like those in the center.
- Substitute Section #16 – flower corner for Section #1 – corner of border, placing a flower in the corner.

Fig. 6-5a. *Celtic Medallion I Layout Diagram.*

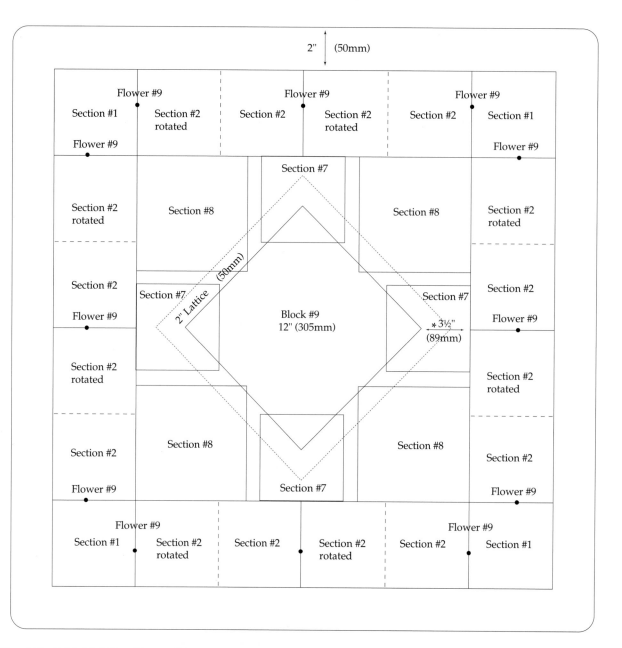

Fig. 6-5b. *Celtic Medallion I Layout Diagram.*

Section #1 – Corner of border – 6" sq. (152mm)

Section #2 – Border knot – 6" x 12" (152mm x 305mm)

Section #7 – Lattice corner – 2" (50mm)

Section #8 – Three loop triangle

Block #9 used in center. Block – 12" sq. (305mm).

Lattice strip – 2" (50mm) wide around block, see Diagram A, page 125.

• – Dots indicate where flowers from Block #9 are placed, each has a flower number next to the dot.
   Dot is 2¼" (57mm) from outside edge of border.

2" (50mm) of background fabric is left around the edge, outside of the border.

* It is 3½" (89mm) from corner of center square to inside edge of border.

Fig. 6-6. *Celtic Medallion I Variation. This variation of Celtic Medallion I uses the same flowers, but the knots are quilted instead of appliquéd.*

Fig. 6-7. *Celtic Medallion II. 40" x 40" (approx. 1m x 1m).*

Celtic Medallion II

Finished size 40" x 40" (approx. 1m x 1m)
See *Figs. 6-7, 6-8a & b, and 6-9*

MATERIALS NEEDED:
    Fabric (45" or 1.14m wide):
      1¼ yards (1.14m) of light gray for background
      1½ yards (1.4m) for backing and hanging sleeve
      ½ yard (46cm) of solid black for bias strips and binding
      ¼ yard (23cm) of each of the following colors:
          silver tricot lamé
          solid medium green
          marbled green
          solid medium red
          solid dark red
          marbled red
          red tricot lamé
          small print black
          black tricot lamé
    Thread to match all colors for the appliqués
    Gray quilting thread
    ¼" (6mm) bias bars

PATTERNS NEEDED:
    Block #8
    Sections #2, 9, 10, and 11
    Diagram A for 3" (76mm) lattice.

INSTRUCTIONS:

Draw out a full-size pattern, using *Fig. 6-8a & b* for placement of the sections and block. Trace the design onto a square of background fabric, using the full width of the fabric. Then make the bias strips and prepare the flower and inset pieces. When pressing the lamé bias strips, use a press cloth or piece of muslin to avoid damaging the lamé. Notice that there are three different blacks and one green used for the bias strips and two different colorations of the flowers and leaves. Using the photo as a guide, baste on the insets and appliqué the bias strips and flowers. After trimming the quilt top to the proper size, cut rounded corners.

QUILTING:

Outline all the appliqué pieces and strips with quilting. The feathers were drawn on the background freehand.

BINDING:

Make a strip of 2½" (64mm) bias for the binding 170" (432 cm) long.

VARIATIONS:
- Use a different block pattern.
- Appliqué the bias strips only, omitting the flowers. (Fig. 6-9, page 51)
- Appliqué the flowers only, substituting the bias strips with quilting or trapunto.
- Change the placement of the insets, use more than one color inset or omit the insets.
- Use one color for all the bias strips.
- Color all the flowers the same.
- Rotate flowers in the border so they face away from the center.

Fig. 6-8a. *Celtic Medallion II Layout Diagram.*

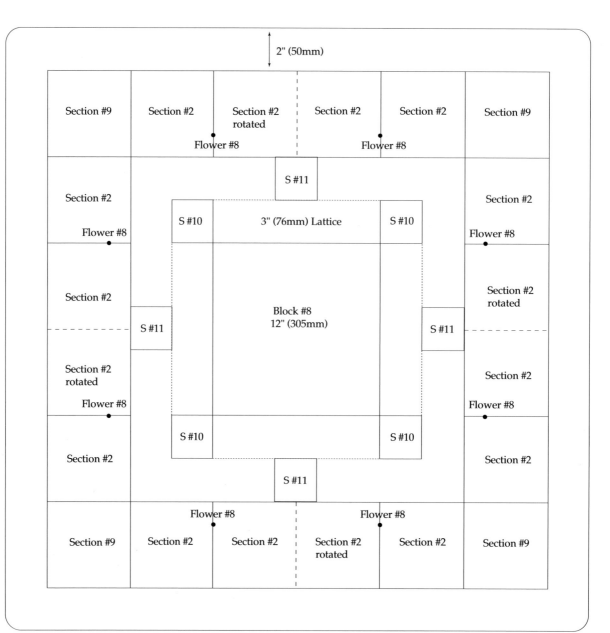

Fig. 6-8b. *Celtic Medallion II Layout Diagram.*

Section #2 – Border knot – 6" x 12" (152mm x 305mm)

Section #2 – ½ Border knot – 6" sq. (152mm)

Section #9 – Corner unit knot

Section #10 – Lattice corner

Section #11 – Lattice intersection

Block #8 used in center. Block – 12" sq. (305mm).

Lattice strip – 3" (76mm) wide around block, see Diagram A, page 125.

• – Dots indicate where flowers from Block #8 are placed, each has a flower number next to dot. Dot is 2¼" (57mm) from inside edge of border.

2" (50mm) of background fabric is left around the edge, outside of the border.

Fig. 6-9. *Celtic Medallion II Variation. This variation of Celtic Medallion II omits the flowers.*

Fig. 6-10. *Celtic Medallion III. 40" x 40" (approx. 1m x 1m).*

Celtic Medallion III

Finished size 40" x 40" (approx. 1m x 1m)
See *Figs. 6-10, 6-11a & b*

MATERIALS NEEDED:

Fabric (45" or 1.14m wide):

1¼ yards (1.14m) of solid light blue for background

1½ yards (1.4m) for backing and hanging sleeve

½ yard (46cm) of blue tricot lamé for bias strips and piping

½ yard (46cm) of solid dark pink for flowers and binding

¼ yard (23cm) of each of the following:

solid medium blue

marbled blue

solid medium green

medium pink chintz

marbled pink

solid neon pink

Thread to match all colors for the appliqués

4½ yards (406.4cm) of cording for making your own piping

Light blue quilting thread

¼" (6mm) bias bar

PATTERNS NEEDED:

Block # 1

Sections #12, 13a, 13b, and 14a & b

Diagram A for 3" (76mm) lattice.

INSTRUCTIONS:

Draw out a full-size pattern, using *Figs. 6-11a & b* for placement of the sections and block. Trace the design onto a square of background fabric, using the full width of the fabric. Then make the bias strips and prepare the flower and inset pieces. When pressing the lamé bias strips, use a press cloth or piece of muslin to avoid damaging the lamé. Notice that there are three different colors of bias strips and two different colorations of the flowers. Using the photo as a guide, baste on the insets and appliqué the bias strips and flowers. After trimming the quilt top to the proper size, cut rounded corners.

QUILTING:

Outline all the appliqué pieces and strips with quilting. The design used for the spaces between appliqués is a large meander pattern that was drawn freehand.

PIPING:

Make the piping by piecing together with mitered seams 1" (25.4mm) wide bias strips of the blue tricot lamé. Fold the strip in half lengthwise with the right side out, insert the cording inside the fold and sew using a zipper foot on your sewing machine. Make 170" (432cm) of the piping. Sew the piping to the quilt with the raw edge of the piping lined up with the edge of the quilt. To join piping, pick out some of the stitches holding the cord inside so that the lamé can be pieced together with a mitered seam. Trim cord so the cut edges butt up against each other. Refold piping and finish sewing to top.

BINDING:

Make a 2½" (64mm) bias strip for the binding 170" (432cm). Sew the binding to the wallhanging using a zipper foot. The piping will appear as a line between the outer border and the binding.

VARIATIONS:
- Use a different block pattern.
- Appliqué the bias strips only, omitting the flowers.
- Appliqué the flowers only, substituting the bias strips with quilting or trapunto.
- Change the placement of the insets, use more than one color inset or omit the insets.
- Use one color for all the bias strips.
- Color all the flowers the same.
- Use flowers from other blocks.
- Reposition the flowers in the border like the ones in Celtic Medallion II (*Fig. 6-8a,* page 49).
- Rotate flowers in the border so they face away from the center.

Fig. 6-11a. *Celtic Medallion III Layout Diagram.*

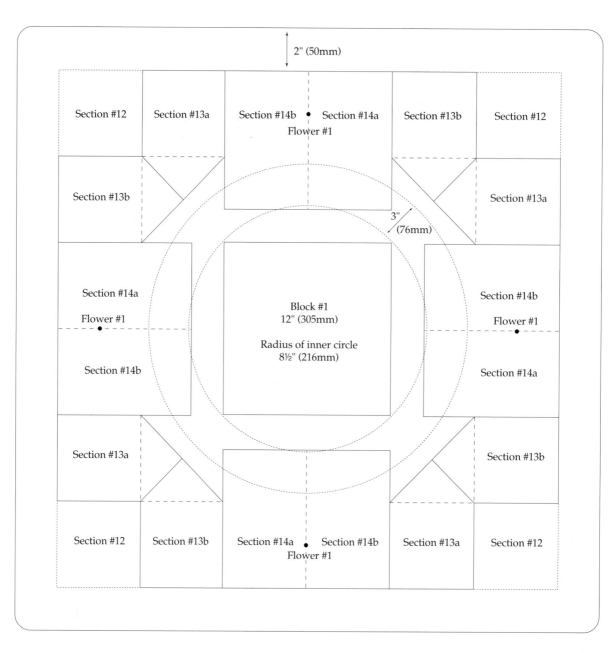

Fig. 6-11b. *Celtic Medallion III Layout Diagram.*

Section #12 – Heart corner unit

Section #13a & b – Loop unit (a and b are mirror images – use separately)

Section #14a & b – Flower loop and lattice intersection (mirrored image joined together)

Block #1 – 12" sq. (305mm)

Lattice strip – 3" (76mm) wide around inner circle, see Diagram A, page 125.

• – Dots indicate where flowers from Block #1 are placed, each has a flower number next to dot. Dot is 2¼" (57mm) from inside edge of border.

2" (50mm) of background fabric is left around the edge, outside of the border.

Fig. 6-12. *Celtic Medallion IV. 40" x 40" (approx. 1m x 1m).*

Celtic Medallion IV

Finished size 40" x 40" (approx. 1m x 1m)
See *Figs. 6-12, 6-13a & b, and 6-14*

MATERIALS NEEDED:
    Fabric (45" or 1.14m wide):
    1¼ yards (1.14m) of periwinkle for background
    1¾ yards (1.6m) of green print for leaves, backing, binding, and hanging sleeve
    ½ yard (46cm) of each of the following colors for bias strips:
        solid light-medium green
        solid medium green
    ¼ yard (23cm) of each of the following for bias strips, insets, and flowers:
        solid medium red
        marbled periwinkle
        solid orange
        orange print
        marbled orange
        yellow print
        solid light green
    Thread to match all colors for the appliqués
    Orange quilting thread
    ¼" (6mm) bias bar

PATTERNS NEEDED:
    Block #6 (adjust flowers to fit inside the diamond lattice)
    Sections #2, 15, 16, 17a & b, 18, and 19
    Diagram A for 3" (76mm) lattice.

INSTRUCTIONS:

Draw out a full-size pattern, using *Figs. 6-13a & b* for placement of the sections and block. Trace the design onto a square of background fabric, using the full width of the fabric. Then make the bias strips and prepare the flower and inset pieces. Notice that there are two different greens and one red used for the bias strips and six different fabrics used for the insets. Using the photo as a guide, baste on the insets, taking care to place the colors correctly, and appliqué the bias strips and flowers. After trimming the quilt top to the proper size, cut rounded corners.

QUILTING:

Outline all the appliqué pieces and strips with quilting. The feathers were drawn in freehand. The diagonal quilted lines are ¾" (19mm) apart. Mark the lines using a ruler and marking pen or pencil, checking the photo for placement.

BINDING:

To make the strip of bias for the binding, piece together random lengths, cut 2½" (64mm) wide, of the green print with shorter lengths of the solid medium green and the solid orange fabric. Sew together to make a strip 170" (432cm) long.

VARIATIONS:

- Use a different block pattern.
- Appliqué the bias strips only, omitting the flowers.
- Appliqué the flowers only, substituting the bias strips with quilting or trapunto.
- Change the placement of the insets, use different color insets, or omit the insets.
- Use one color for all the bias strips.
- Use different colorations for the flower.
- Use flowers from other blocks. (Fig. 6-14, page 62).
- Rotate flowers with border so they face away from the center.
- Substitute Section #1 – corner of the border for Section #16 – flower corner.

Fig. 6-13a. *Celtic Medallion IV Layout Diagram.*

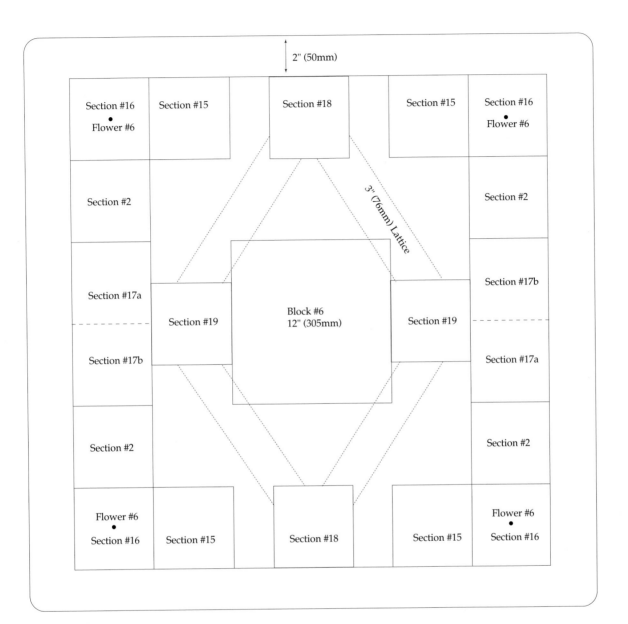

Fig. 6-13b. *Celtic Medallion IV Layout Diagram.*

   Section #2 – ½ Border knot – 6"sq. (152mm)

   Section #15 – Loop knot

   Section #16 – Flower corner

   Section #17a & b – Fancy knot

   Section #18 – Point of diamond

   Section #19 – Intersection of diamond

Block #6 used in center, adjust flowers to fit inside diamond. Block – 12" sq. (305mm).

Lattice – 3" (76mm) wide connecting Section #18 to #19, see Diagram A, page 125.

• – Dots indicate where flowers from Block #6 are placed, each has a flower number next to dot. Dot
   is 2¼" (57mm) from inside edges of Section #16.

2" (50mm) of background fabric is left around the edge, outside of the border.

Fig. 6-14. *Celtic Medallion IV Variation. This variation of Celtic Medallion IV uses a different flower from Block #5 variation.*

Fig. 6-15. *Symphony. 27" x 27" (approx. 68.5cm x 68.5cm).*

Symphony

Finished size 27" x 27" (68.5cm x 68.5cm)
See *Figs. 6-15 and 6-16a & b*

   This wallhanging was made by Patty Oliver-Matz of Weaverville, California, for the Mt. Village Quilter's Guild Challenge. She has graciously allowed me to include the pattern for Symphony in this book. Patty took my class in February 1993, and went on to make changes in the block she started in class for her guild quilt challenge.

MATERIALS NEEDED:
   Fabric (45" or 1.14m wide):
   ⅜ yard (34.2cm) of cream print for block background
   ⅞ yard (80cm) for backing and hanging sleeve
   ½ yard (46cm) of black print for leaves, bias strips, and second border
   ⅛ yard (11.4cm) of tan small print for petals and first border
   1 yard (92cm) of tan large print for insets and third border
   Scrap of dark purple print approx. 3" (76mm) square for flower centers
   Scrap of marbled lavender approx. 6" (152mm) square for the extra leaves
   Thread to match all colors for the appliqués
   Gold metallic thread for quilting
   ¼" (6mm) bias bar

PATTERNS NEEDED:
      Block #1 - variation
      Sections #20, 21a, and 21b.

INSTRUCTIONS:

Draw out a full-size pattern, using *Figs. 6-16a & b* for placement of the sections and block. When you cut your fabric for the block background and three borders, don't forget to add seam allowances. Trace the design on the block fabric. Then make the bias strips and prepare the flower and inset pieces. Using the photo as a guide, baste on the insets and appliqué the bias strips and flowers. After the block is finished, piece the rest of the wallhanging, mitering the border corners (*Fig. 5-1*, page 30). Trace the design on the outer border and appliqué the border design. Trim the quilt top to the proper size.

QUILTING:

Outline all the appliqué pieces and strips with quilting and quilt along the border seams with gold metallic thread.

BINDING:

Make a piece of 2½" (64mm) bias for the binding 112" (285cm) long. Sew the binding to the quilt, mitering the corners.

VARIATIONS:
• Use a different block pattern.
• Appliqué the bias strips only, omitting the flowers.
• Change the placement of the insets, use more than one color inset, or omit the insets.
• Use more than one color for the bias strips.

Fig. 6-16a. *Symphony Layout Diagram.*

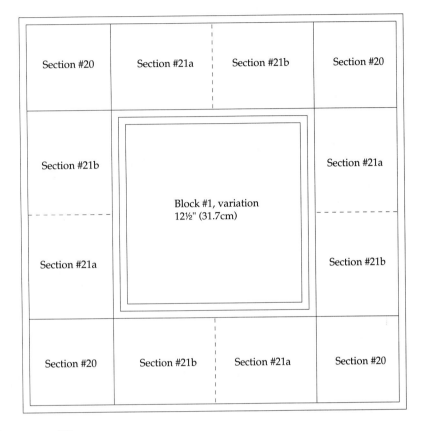

Fig. 6-16b. *Symphony Layout Diagram*

Section #20 – Swirl corner

Section #21a – Side knot

Section #21b – Side knot

Block #1 variation – 12½" sq. (31.7cm) add seam allowances

First border is ½" (12mm) add seam allowances

Second border is ½" (12mm) add seam allowances

Third border is 6" (15.2cm) add seam allowances

More Variations

Here are more ideas for using the blocks and sections in this book.

After redesigning the border for each wallhanging, I realized that these borders would also look good with the original quilt center from the Celtic Orchids sampler quilt (*Fig. 7-1a & b*, pages 69–70). Also, because all the patterns are based on a 6" (15.2cm) grid, it is easy to expand the original quilt design to make a larger quilts (*Figs. 7-2a & b*, pages 71–72). If you want a rectangular version of Celtic Orchids, use the original border top and bottom, and the larger version for the sides. This would use 12 blocks in the center and finish 78" x 90" (1982mm x 2286mm). The spacing between the lattice and the top and bottom will be 6" (152mm), between the lattice and the sides will be 4½" (114mm).

I also designed four large quilts based on each of the wallhangings. Celtic Medallion I became Interlace on Point (*Figs. 7-3a & b*, page 73–74). Celtic Medallion II changed into Interlace Squared (*Figs. 7-4a & b*, page 75–76). Celtic Medallion III became Interlace in the Round (*Figs. 7-5a & b*, page 77–78). This design reminds me of the Double Wedding Ring, a traditional pattern I haven't attempted yet. Last, Celtic Medallion IV is now Interlaced Diamonds (*Figs. 7-6a & b*, pages 79–80).

If you want to make your own variation of one of these quilts, feel free to change these layouts even more. If you can make photocopies of the scale diagrams, these can be cut apart and reassembled in a new layout. Remember, the variations discussed in earlier chapters can also be applied to these four larger designs. For example, *Fig. 7-7*, page 81, shows Interlace in the Round as a sampler quilt using all nine different appliqué blocks. Use your imagination!

I really enjoy doing interlaced scrollwork. I have ideas for many more variations of the patterns in this book and as I research the various design styles, the possibilities from those sources also seem to be endless. I'm saving these ideas for my next book!

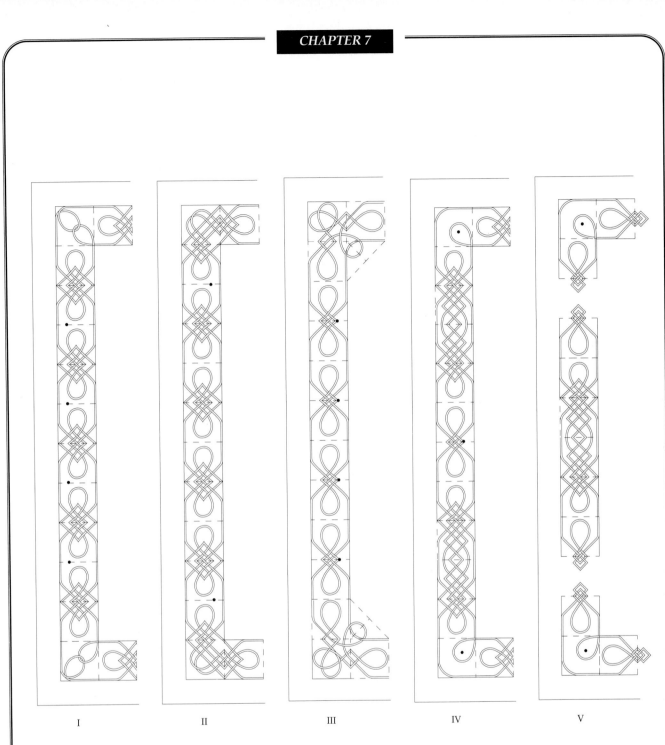

I II III IV V

Fig. 7-1a. *Alternate Borders for Celtic Orchids*

• – Dots indicate where flowers are placed. Dot is 2¼" (57mm) from inside or outside edge of border, depending on which way the flowers are oriented.

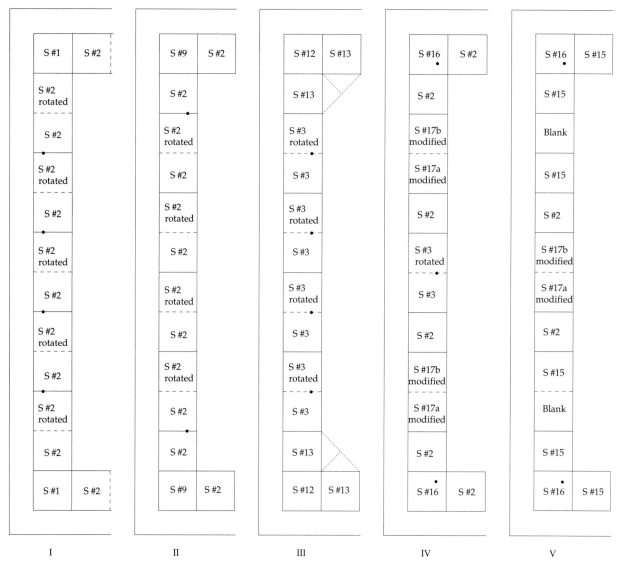

| I | II | III | IV | V |

Fig. 7-1b. *Alternate Borders for Celtic Orchids*

• – Dots indicate where flowers are placed. Dot is 2¼" (57mm) from inside or outside edge of border, depending on which way the flowers are oriented. These borders can be adjusted to fit the large size of Celtic Orchids (Fig. 7-2a). In I add another S #2 and S #2 rotated. In II add a S #2 and S #2 rotated. In III add S #3 and S #3 rotated. In IV add another S #3 and S #3 rotated next to S #3 and S #3 rotated. In V make the blank 6" (15.2cm) squares into 6" x 12" (15.2cm x 30.4cm) blanks.

Fig. 7-2a. *Celtic Orchids, Layout Diagram, larger size. 90" x 90" (2286mm x 2286mm).*

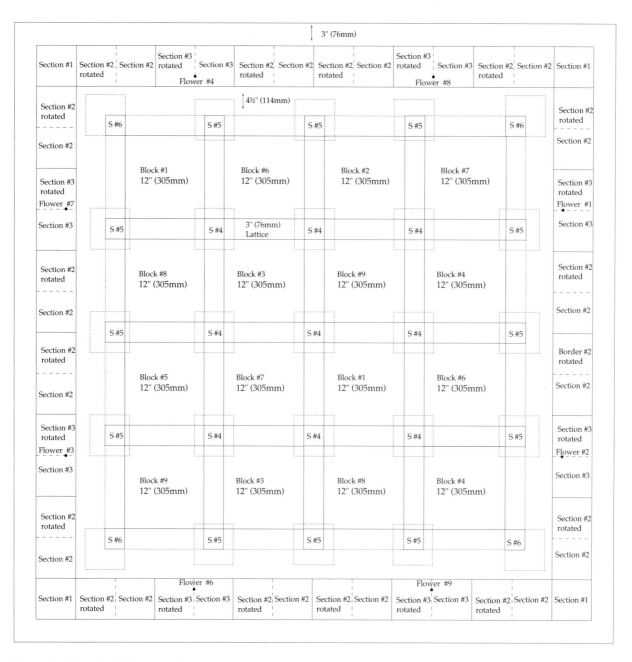

Fig. 7-2b. *Celtic Orchid, Layout Diagram, larger size.*

Section #1 – Corner of border

Section #2 – Border knot

Section #3 – Border knot with flower

Section #4 – Intersection knot

Section #5 – Edge knot

Section #6 – Corner knot

Blocks #1 – #9 – 12" sq. (305mm)

• – Dots indicate where flowers are placed, each has a flower number next to dot. Dot is 2¼" (57mm) from inside edge of border.

3" Lattice strip (76mm) see Diagram A, page 125.

3" (76mm) of background fabric is left around the edge, outside of the border.

Fig. 7-3a. *Interlace On Point Layout Diagram. 90" x 90" (2286mm x 2286mm).*

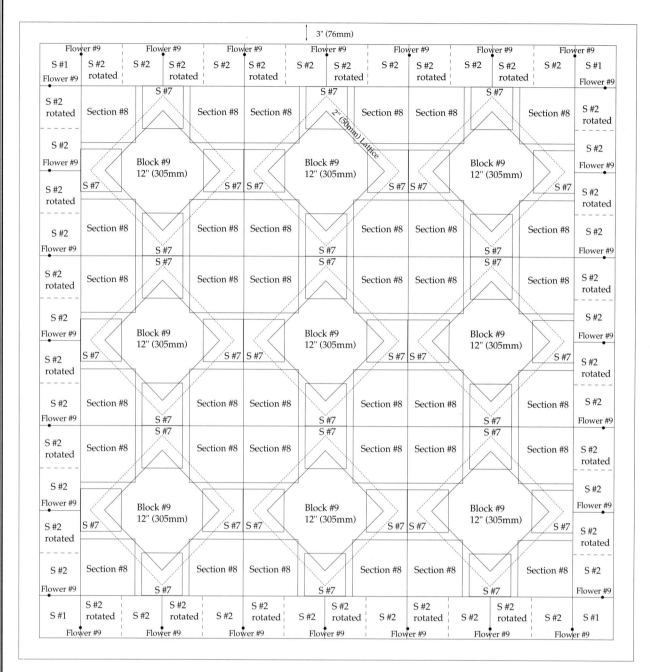

Fig. 7-3b. *Interlace On Point Layout Diagram*

Section #1 – Corner of border

Section #2 – Border knot

Section #7 – 2" Lattice corner

Section #8 – Three loop triangle

Block #9 – 12" sq. (305mm)

- • – Dots indicate where flowers are placed, each has a flower number next to dot. Dot is 2¼" (57mm) from outside edge of border.

2" Lattice strip (50mm) around blocks, see Diagram A, page 125.

3" (76mm) of background fabric is left around the edge, outside of the border.

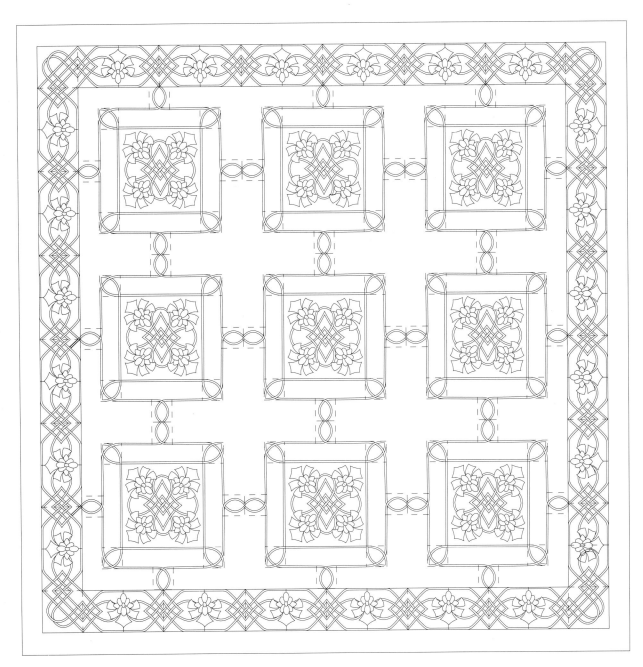

Fig. 7-4a. *Interlace Squared Layout Diagram. 90" x 90" (approx. 2286mm x 2286mm).*

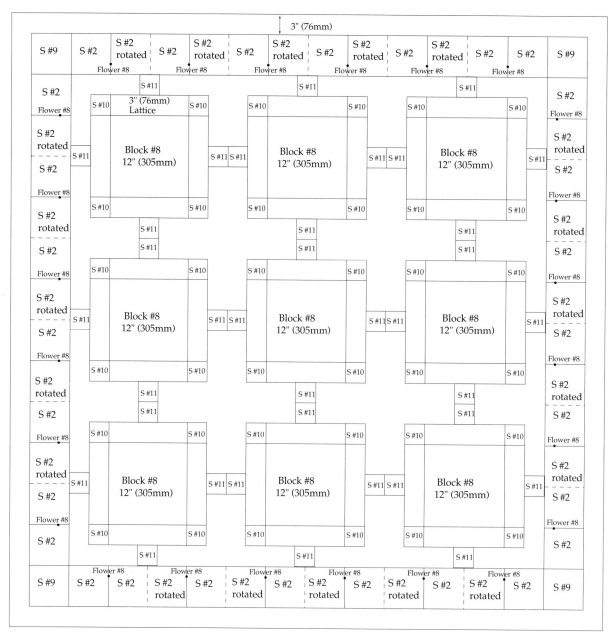

Fig. 7-4b. *Interlace Squared Layout Diagram*

Section #2 – Border knot

Section #2 – ½ Border knot

Section #9 – Corner knot

Section #10 – Lattice corner

Section #11 – Lattice intersection

Block #8 – 12" sq. (305mm)

• – Dots indicate where flowers are placed, each has a flower number next to dot. Dot is 2¼" (57mm) from inside edge of border.

3" Lattice strip (76mm) around blocks, see Diagram A, page 125.

3" (76mm) of background fabric is left around the edge, outside of the border.

Fig. 7-5a. *Interlace In The Round Layout Diagram. 90" x 90" (approx. 2286mm x 2286mm).*

Fig. 7-5b. *Interlace In The Round Layout Diagram*

Section #12 – Heart corner unit

Sections #13a & b – Loop unit

Sections #14a & b – Flower loop and lattice intersection (a & b are mirror images)

Sections #14c & d – Lattice intersection only

Block #1 – 12" sq. (305mm)

• – Dots indicate where flowers are placed, each has a flower number next to dot. Dot is 2¼" (57mm) from inside edge of border.

Radius of inner circle is 8½" (216mm).

3" (76mm) lattice around inner circle.

3" (76mm) of background fabric is left around the edge, outside of the border.

Fig. 7-6a. *Interlaced Diamonds Layout Diagram. 90" x 90" (approx. 2286mm x 2286mm).*

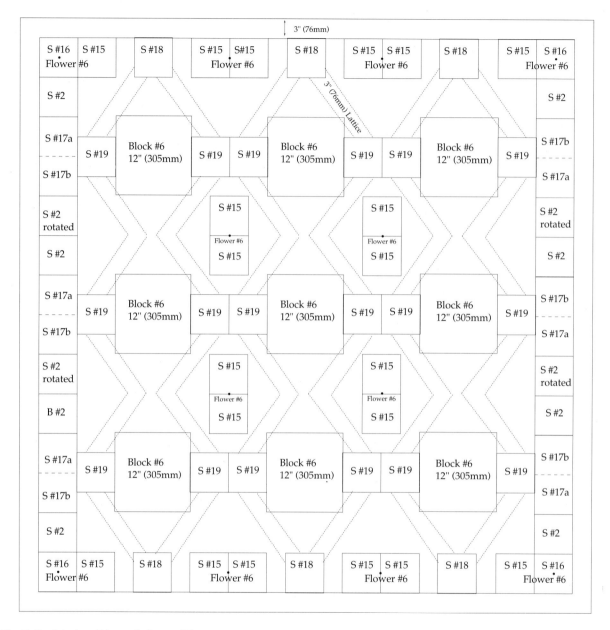

Fig. 7-6b. *Interlace Diamonds Layout Diagram*

Section #2 – ½ Border knot

Section #15 – One loop knot

Section #16 – Flower corner

Section #17 – Fancy knot (a & b are mirror images)

Section #18 – Point of diamond

Section #19 – Intersection of diamond

Block #6 – 12" sq. (305mm)

3" (76mm) lattice connects Sections #18 to #19, see Diagram A, page 125

• – Dots indicate where flowers are placed, each has a flower number next to dot. Dot is 2¼" (57mm) from inside edge of border and inside edges of Section #16.

3" (76mm) of background fabric is left around the edge, outside of the border.

Fig. 7-7. *Interlace In The Round Layout Diagram. 90" x 90" (approx. 2286mm x 2286mm).*

Same as figure 7-6a, but use all nine flower blocks.

Block Patterns

center   6" square (152mm)

Block #1

12" finished size (305mm)

¼ of design – copy 4 times, trim along dotted lines, matching centers, then tape
  together.

Pieces are numbered in the order that they need to be appliquéd.

pattern guide

center   6" square (152mm)

Block #1 Variation

Variation by Patty Oliver-Matz of Weaverville, California

12" finished size (305mm)

¼ of design – copy 4 times, trim along dotted lines, matching centers, then tape together.

Pieces are numbered in the order that they need to be appliquéd.

pattern guide

center   6" square (152mm)

pattern guide

Block #2

12" finished size (305mm)

¼ of design – copy 4 times, trim along dotted lines, matching centers, then tape together.

Pieces are numbered in the order that they need to be appliquéd.

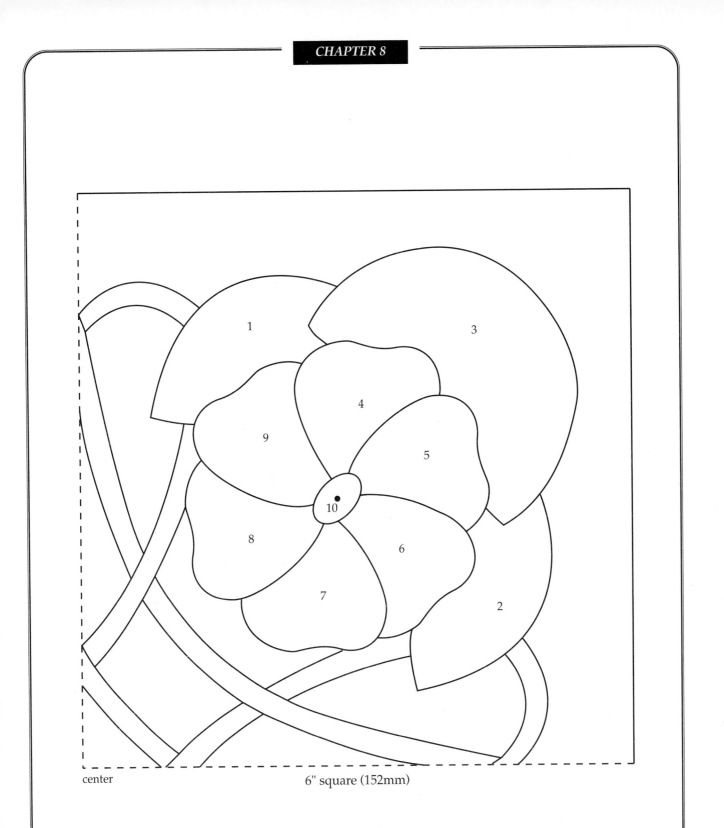

center   6" square (152mm)

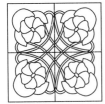

Block #2 Variation

12" finished size (305mm)

Variation used in sample blocks.

¼ of design – copy 4 times, trim along dotted lines, matching centers, then tape together.

pattern guide

Pieces are numbered in the order that they need to be appliquéd.

center   6" square (152mm)

Block #3

12" finished size (305mm)

¼ of design – copy 4 times, trim along dotted lines, matching centers, then tape
     together.

Pieces are numbered in the order that they need to be appliquéd.

pattern guide

center

6" square (152mm)

pattern guide

Block #4

12" finished size (305mm)

¼ of design – copy 4 times, trim along dotted lines, matching centers, then tape
together.

Pieces are numbered in the order that they need to be appliquéd.

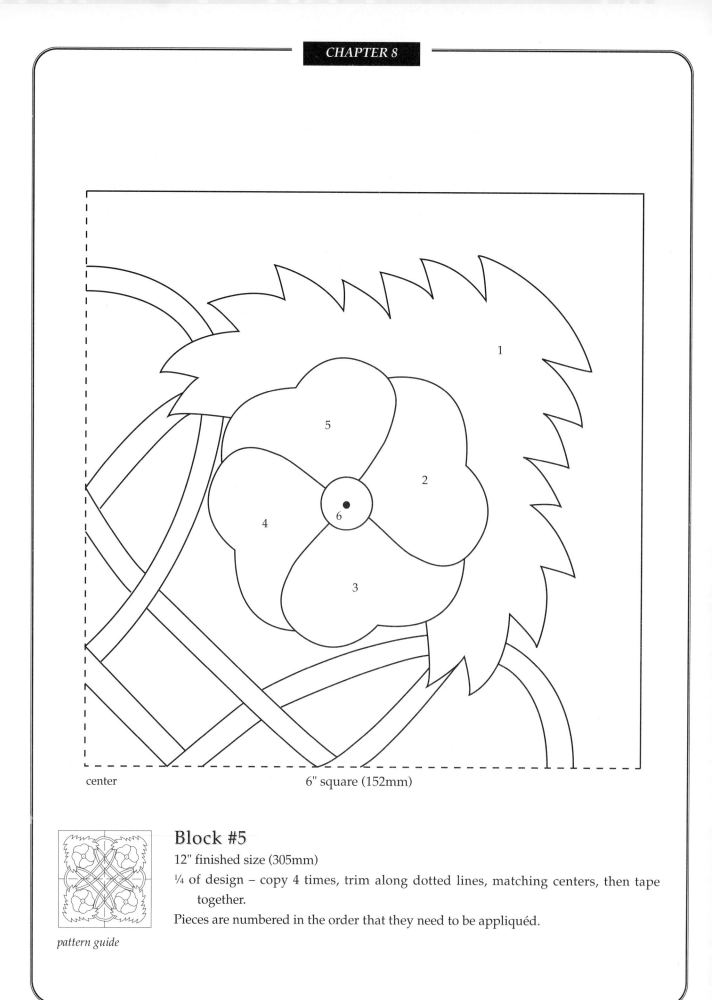

center   6" square (152mm)

Block #5

12" finished size (305mm)

¼ of design – copy 4 times, trim along dotted lines, matching centers, then tape
  together.

Pieces are numbered in the order that they need to be appliquéd.

pattern guide

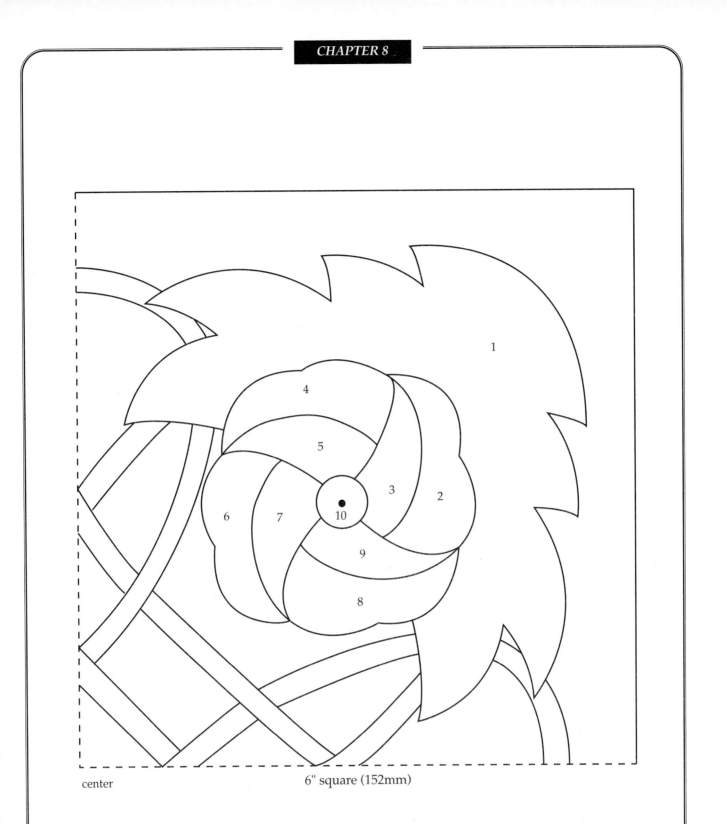

center   6" square (152mm)

pattern guide

Block #5 Variation

12" finished size (305mm)

Variation used in sample block.

¼ of design – copy 4 times, trim along dotted lines, matching centers, then tape
    together.

Pieces are numbered in the order that they need to be appliquéd.

center

A

B

6" square (152mm)

Block #6 part 2	Block #6 part 1
Block #6 part 1	Block #6 part 2

assembly guide

Block #6 Part 1

12" finished size (305mm)

¼ of design – copy 2 times, trim along dotted lines, following assembly guide match centers, then tape together with A and B lines matching.

Pieces are numbered in the order that they need to be appliquéd.

center

A

B

6" square (152mm)

pattern guide

Block #6 Part 2

12" finished size (305mm)

¹¼ of design – copy 2 times, trim along dotted lines, following assembly guide match
centers, then tape together with A and B lines matching.

Pieces are numbered in the order that they need to be appliquéd.

6" square (152mm)

Block #7 part 2	Block #7 part 1
Block #7 part 1	Block #7 part 2

assembly guide

Block #7 Part 1

12" finished size (305mm)

¼ of design – copy 2 times, trim along dotted lines, following assembly guide match centers, then tape together with A and B lines matching.

Pieces are numbered in the order that they need to be appliquéd.

center

A

B

8

9

10

1

4

7

6

5

3

2

6" square (152mm)

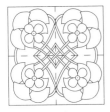

pattern guide

Block #7 Part 2

12" finished size (305mm)

¼ of design – copy 2 times, trim along dotted lines, following assembly guide match
   centers, then tape together with A and B lines matching.

Pieces are numbered in the order that they need to be appliquéd.

center

A

B

6" square (152mm)

Block #8 part 2	Block #8 part 1
Block #8 part 1	Block #8 part 2

assembly guide

Block #8 Part 1

12" finished size (305mm)

¼ of design – copy 2 times, trim along dotted lines, following assembly guide match centers, then tape together with A and B lines matching.

Pieces are numbered in the order that they need to be appliquéd.

center

A

B

1

13   8   7

14

9   10

2

6   12

11

5

4

3

6" square (152mm)

Block #8 Part 2

12" finished size (305mm)

¼ of design – copy 2 times, trim along dotted lines, following assembly guide match
    centers, then tape together with A and B lines matching.

Pieces are numbered in the order that they need to be appliquéd.

pattern guide

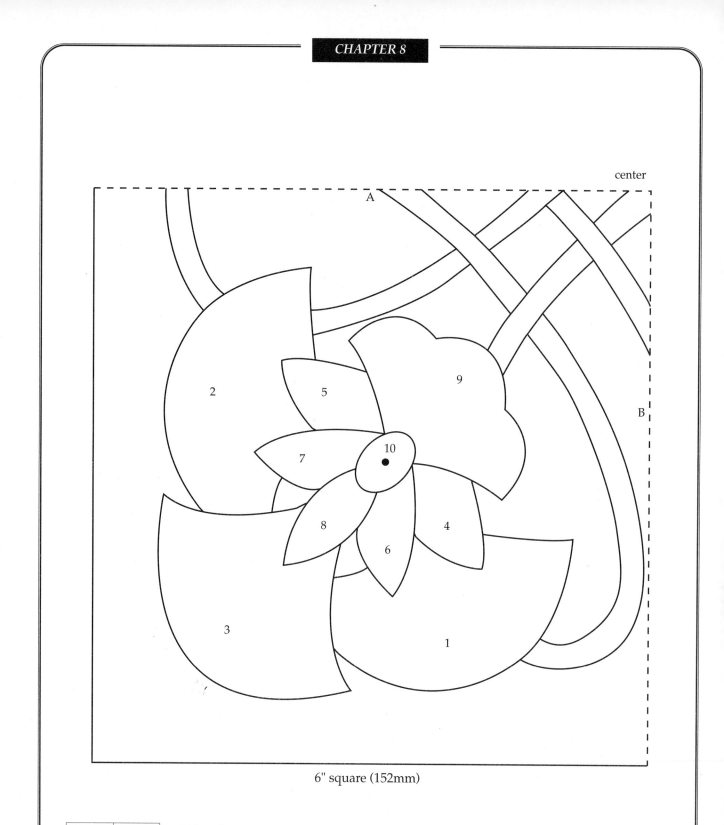

center

A

B

6" square (152mm)

Block #9 part 2	Block #9 part 1
Block #9 part 1	Block #9 part 2

assembly guide

Block #9 Part 1

12" finished size (305mm)

¼ of design – copy 2 times, trim along dotted lines, following assembly guide match centers, then tape together with A and B lines matching.

Pieces are numbered in the order that they need to be appliquéd.

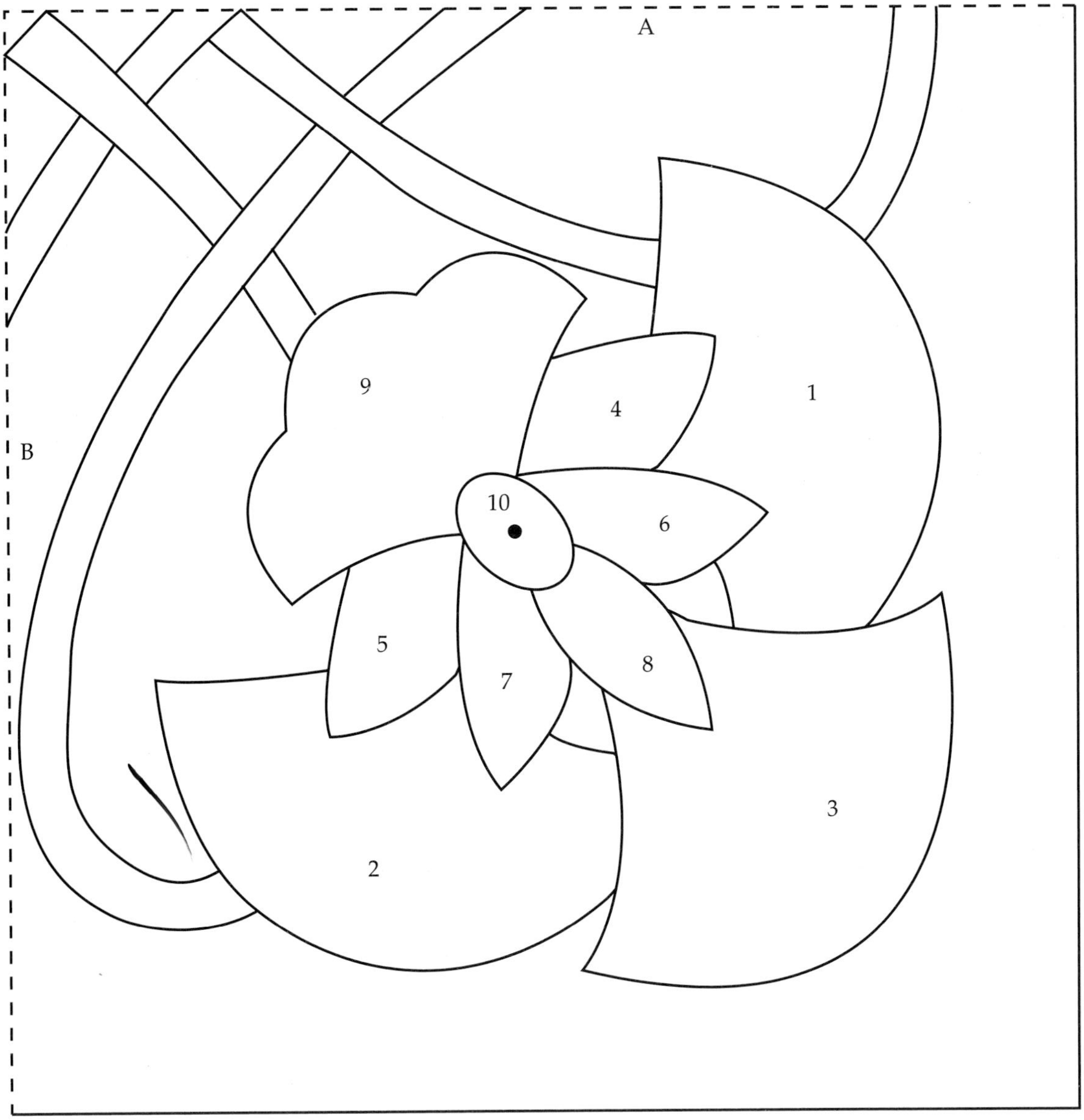

center

A

B

10

9

4

1

6

5

7

8

2

3

6" square (152mm)

Block #9 Part 2

12" finished size (305mm)

¼ of design – copy 2 times, trim along dotted lines, following assembly guide match
   centers, then tape together with A and B lines matching.

Pieces are numbered in the order that they need to be appliquéd.

pattern guide

Section Patterns

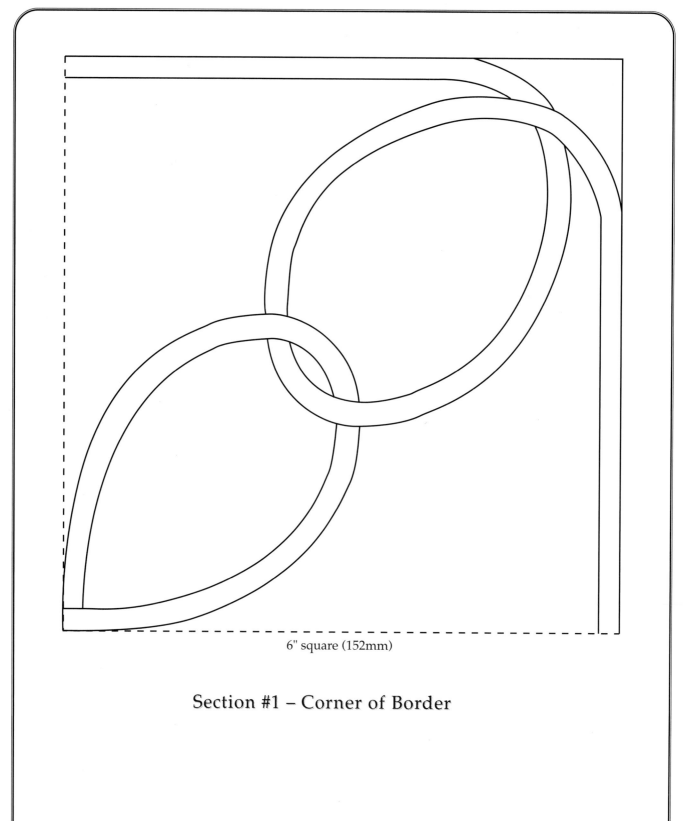

6" square (152mm)

Section #1 – Corner of Border

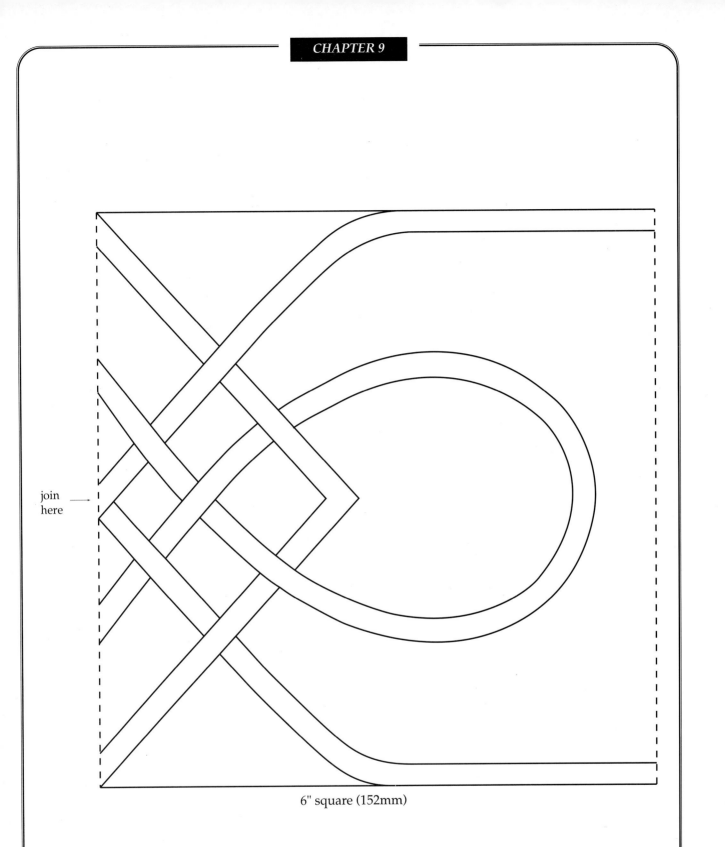

join
here →

6" square (152mm)

Section #2 – Border Knot

Pattern is for ½ of Border #2. Join two halves together forming the knot with loops on either side. Copy this half twice and rotate loop to the left side.

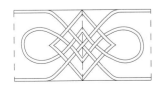

pattern guide

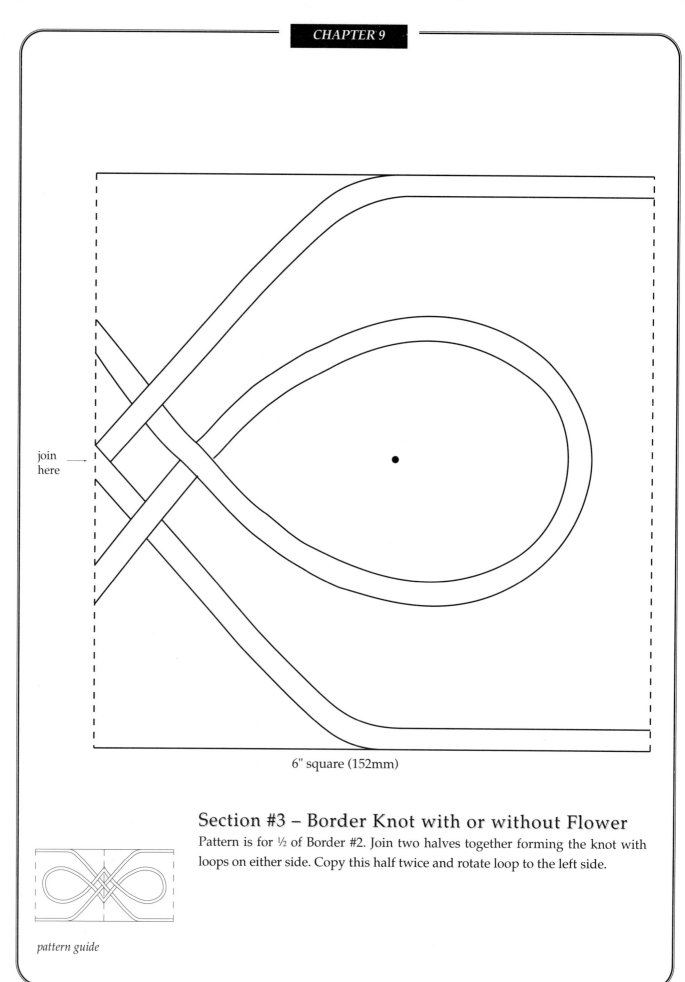

join
here →

6" square (152mm)

Section #3 – Border Knot with or without Flower

Pattern is for ½ of Border #2. Join two halves together forming the knot with
loops on either side. Copy this half twice and rotate loop to the left side.

pattern guide

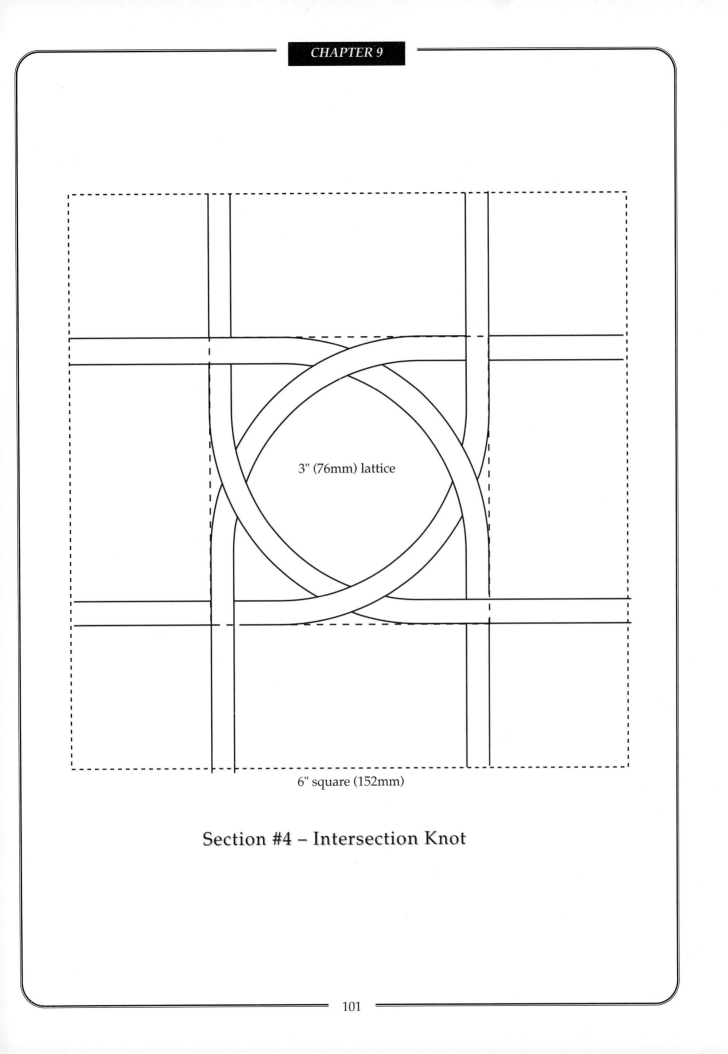

3" (76mm) lattice

6" square (152mm)

Section #4 – Intersection Knot

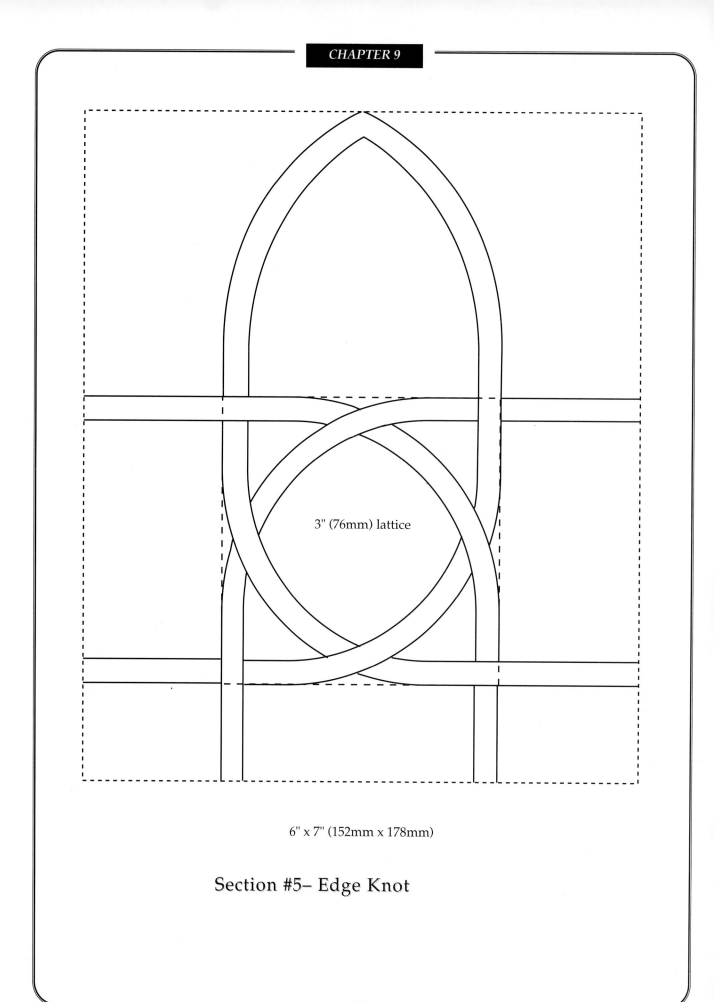

3" (76mm) lattice

6" x 7" (152mm x 178mm)

Section #5– Edge Knot

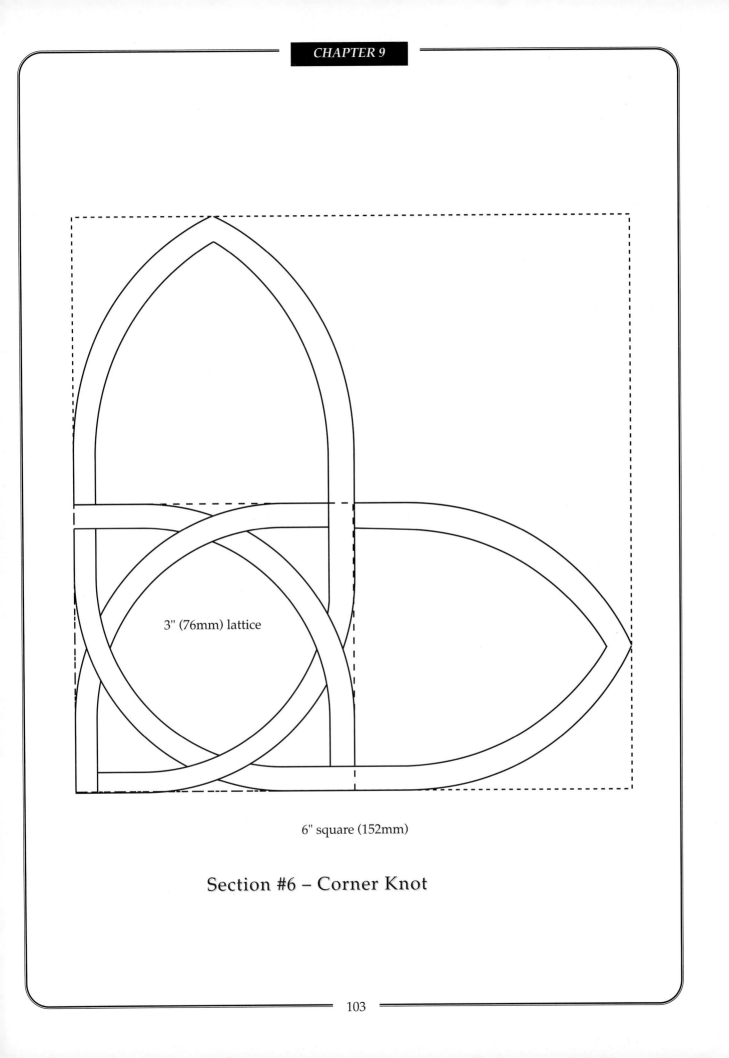

3" (76mm) lattice

6" square (152mm)

Section #6 – Corner Knot

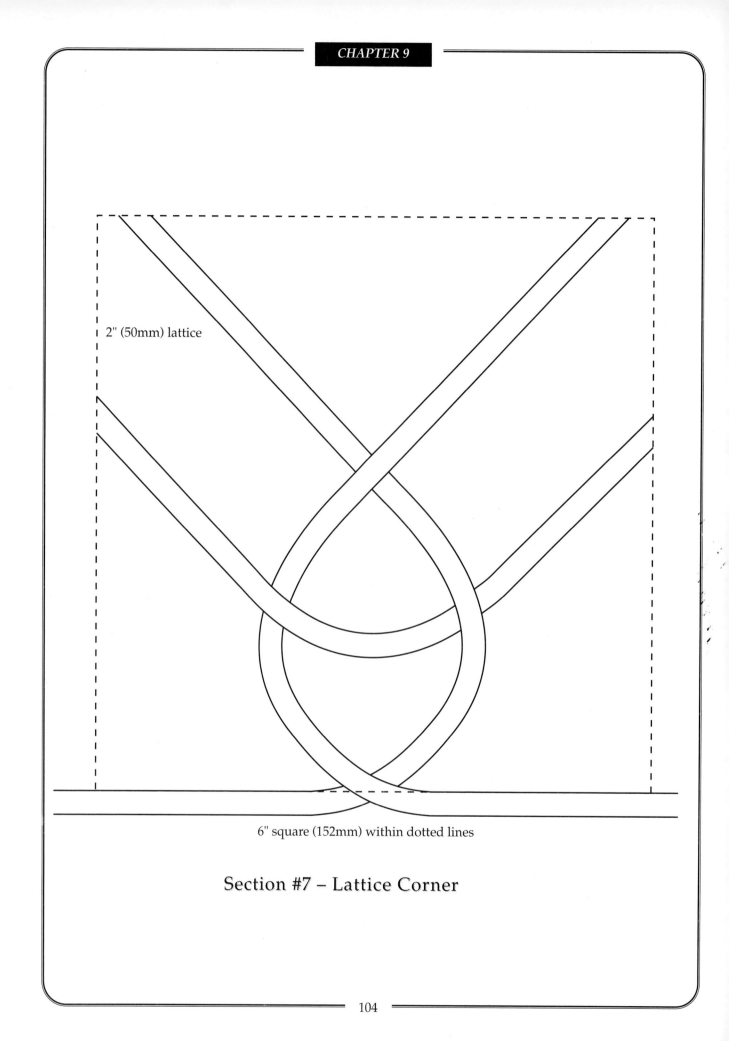

2" (50mm) lattice

6" square (152mm) within dotted lines

Section #7 – Lattice Corner

6" (152mm)

Section #8 – Three Loop Triangle

6" square (152mm)

Section #9 – Corner Unit Knot

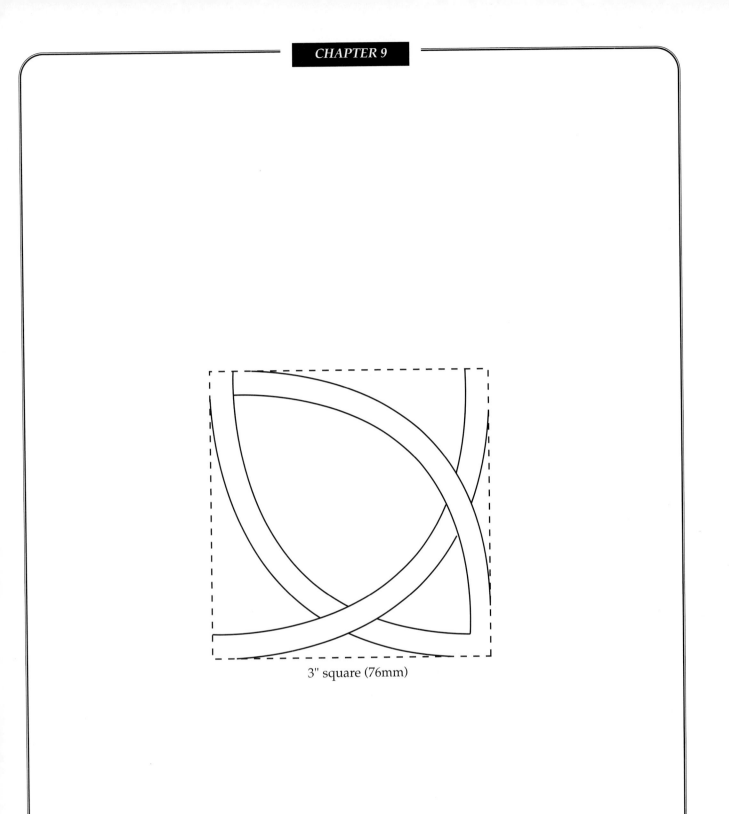

3" square (76mm)

Section #10 – Lattice Corner

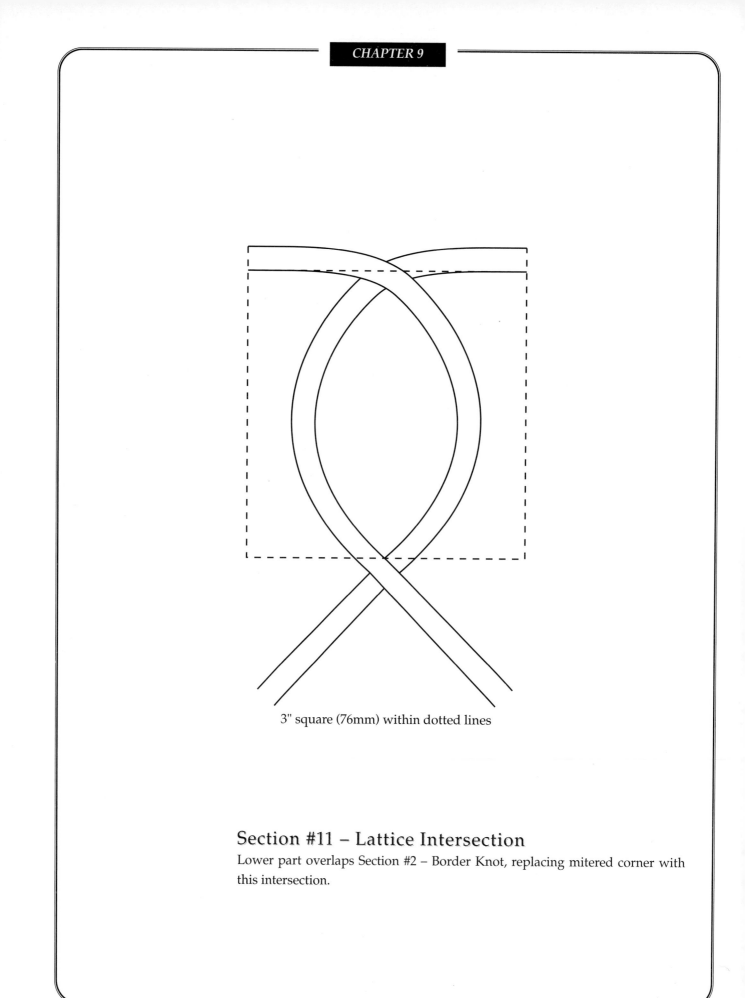

3" square (76mm) within dotted lines

Section #11 – Lattice Intersection

Lower part overlaps Section #2 – Border Knot, replacing mitered corner with this intersection.

6" square (152mm)

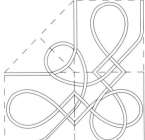

Section #12 – Heart Corner Unit
Pattern guide has Section #12 shown with Sections #13a and #13b.

pattern guide

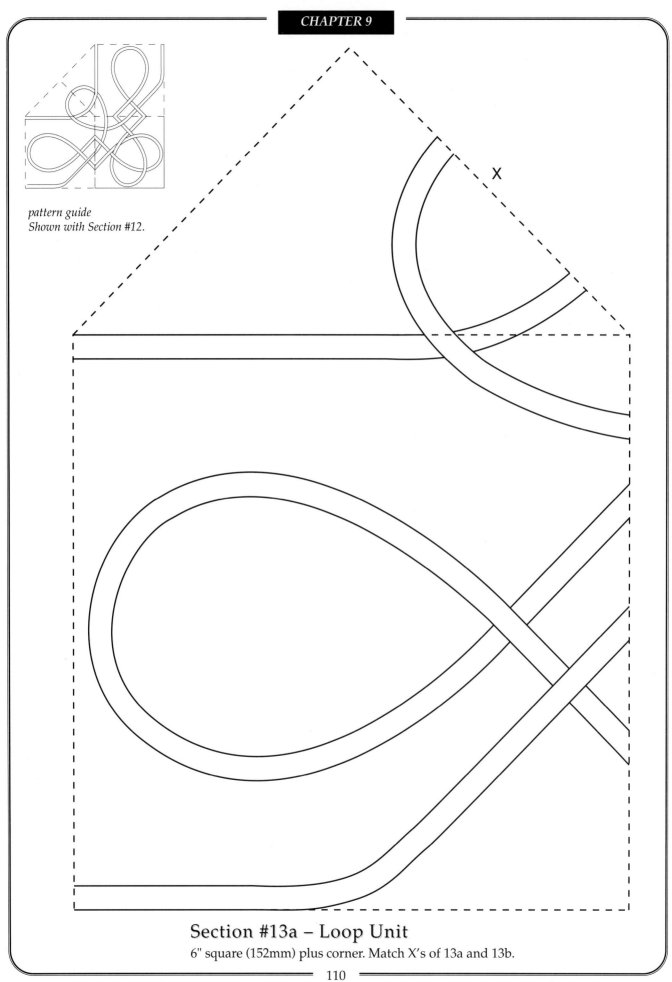

pattern guide
Shown with Section #12.

Section #13a – Loop Unit

6" square (152mm) plus corner. Match X's of 13a and 13b.

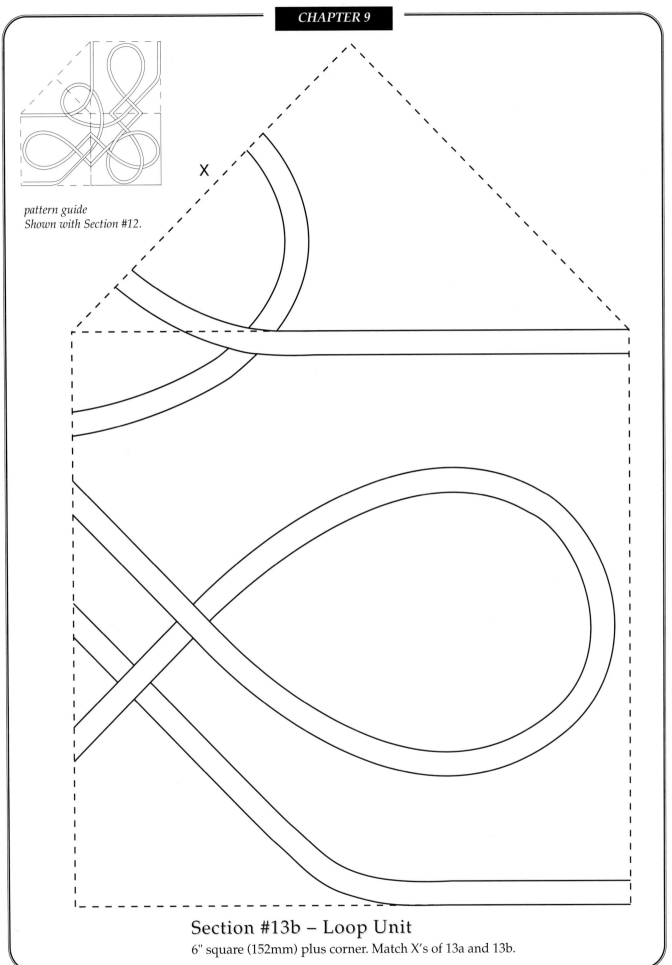

pattern guide
Shown with Section #12.

X

Section #13b – Loop Unit

6" square (152mm) plus corner. Match X's of 13a and 13b.

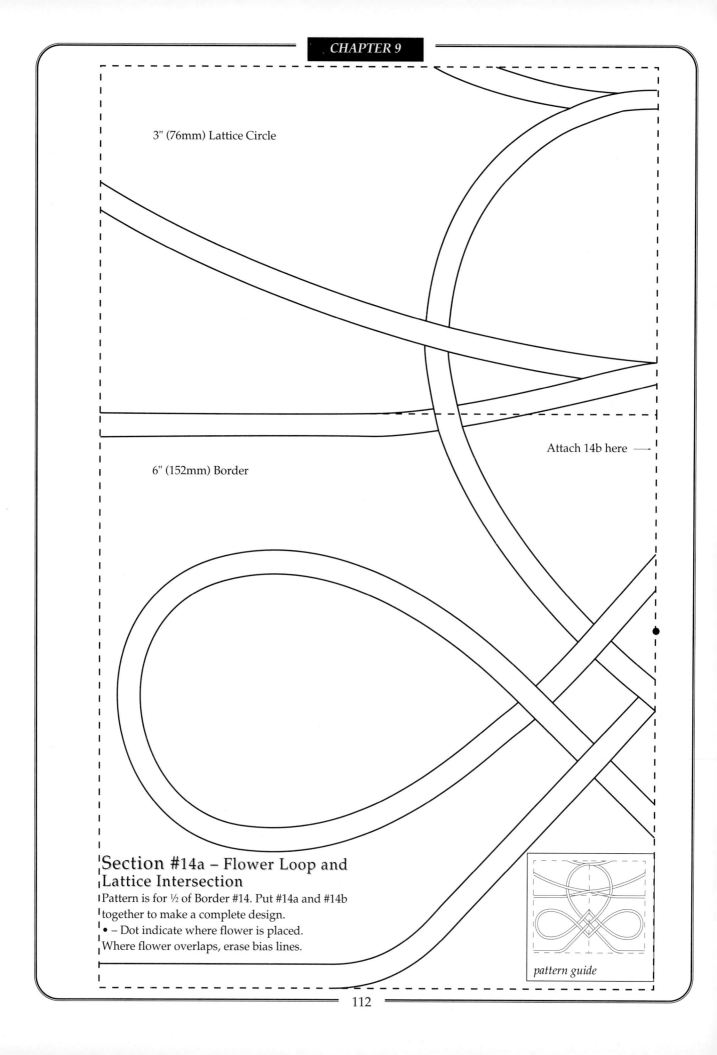

3" (76mm) Lattice Circle

6" (152mm) Border

Attach 14b here ⟶

Section #14a – Flower Loop and Lattice Intersection

Pattern is for ½ of Border #14. Put #14a and #14b together to make a complete design.
• – Dot indicate where flower is placed.
Where flower overlaps, erase bias lines.

pattern guide

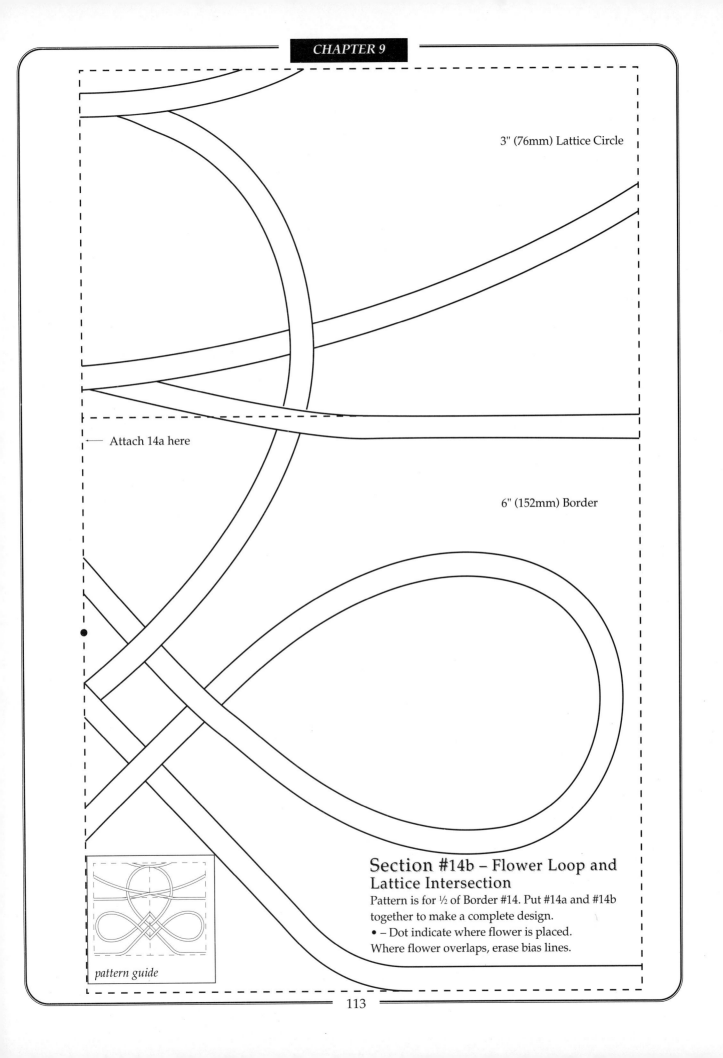

3" (76mm) Lattice Circle

← Attach 14a here

6" (152mm) Border

Section #14b – Flower Loop and Lattice Intersection

Pattern is for ½ of Border #14. Put #14a and #14b together to make a complete design.

• – Dot indicate where flower is placed.

Where flower overlaps, erase bias lines.

pattern guide

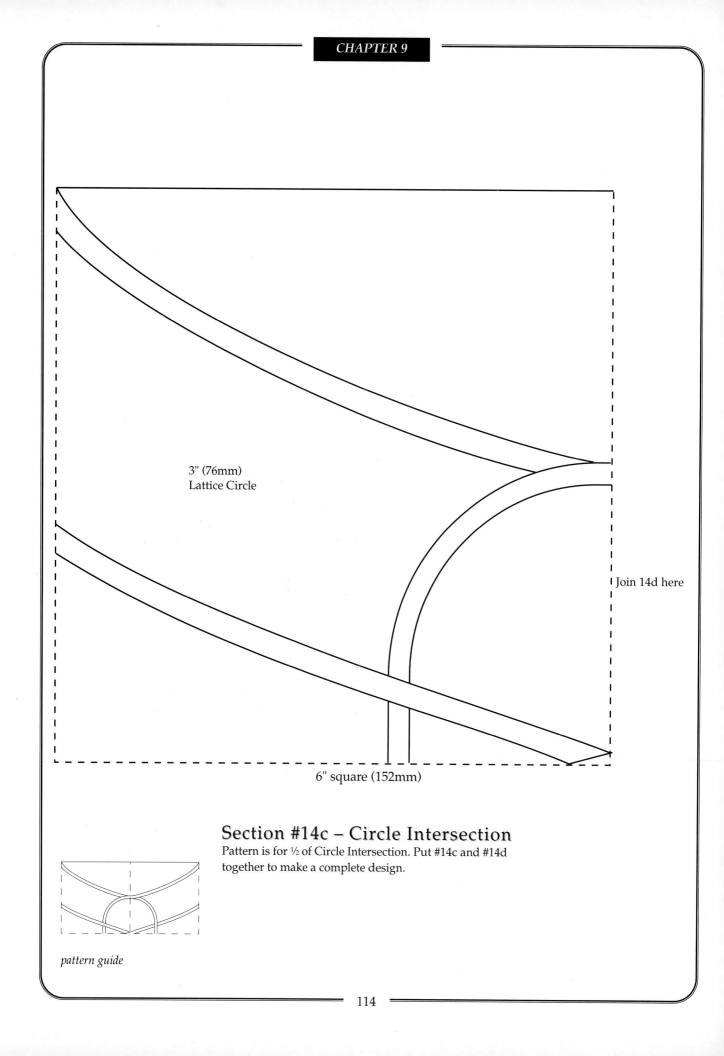

3" (76mm)
Lattice Circle

Join 14d here

6" square (152mm)

Section #14c – Circle Intersection

Pattern is for ½ of Circle Intersection. Put #14c and #14d
together to make a complete design.

pattern guide

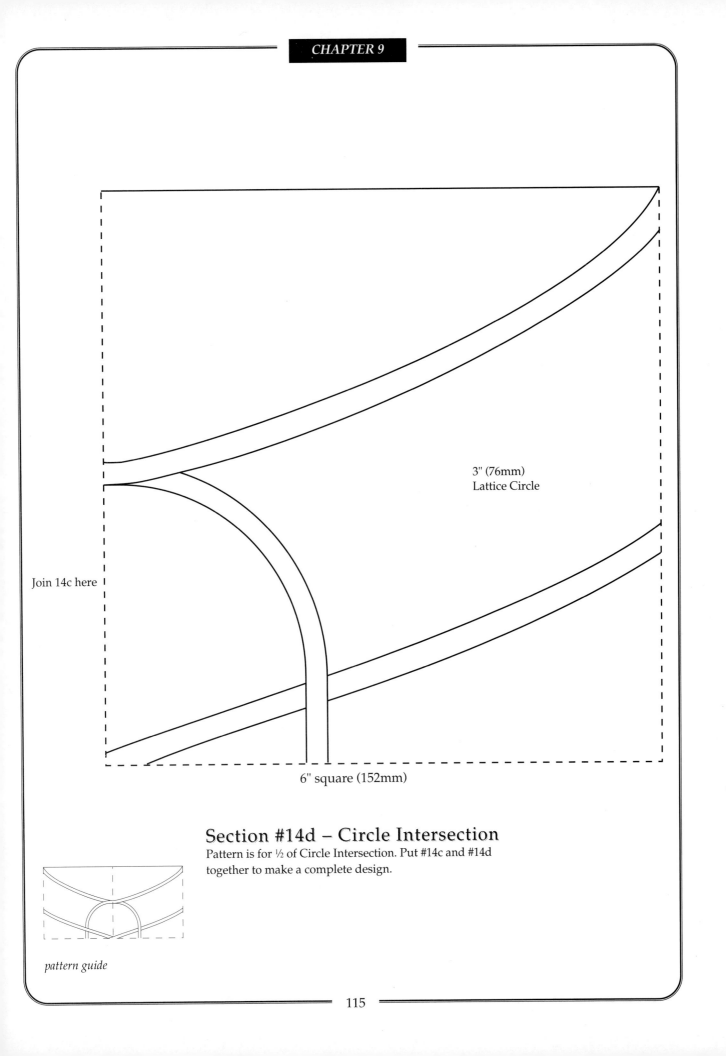

3" (76mm)
Lattice Circle

Join 14c here

6" square (152mm)

Section #14d – Circle Intersection

Pattern is for ½ of Circle Intersection. Put #14c and #14d
together to make a complete design.

pattern guide

6" square (152mm)

Section #15 – One Loop Knot

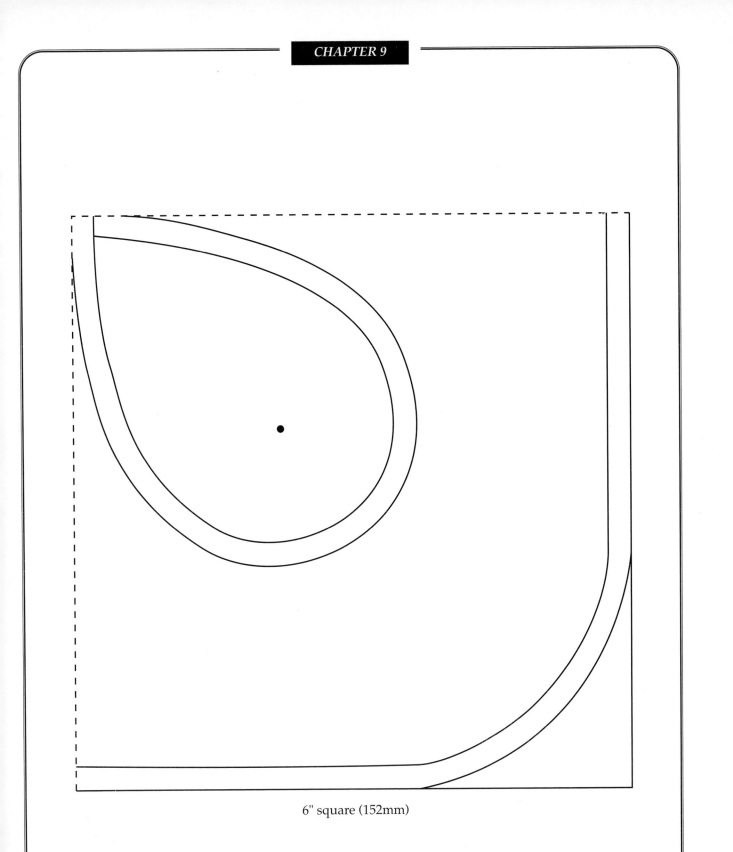

6" square (152mm)

Section #16 – Flower Corner

• – Dot indicates where flower is placed. Where flower overlaps erase bias lines.

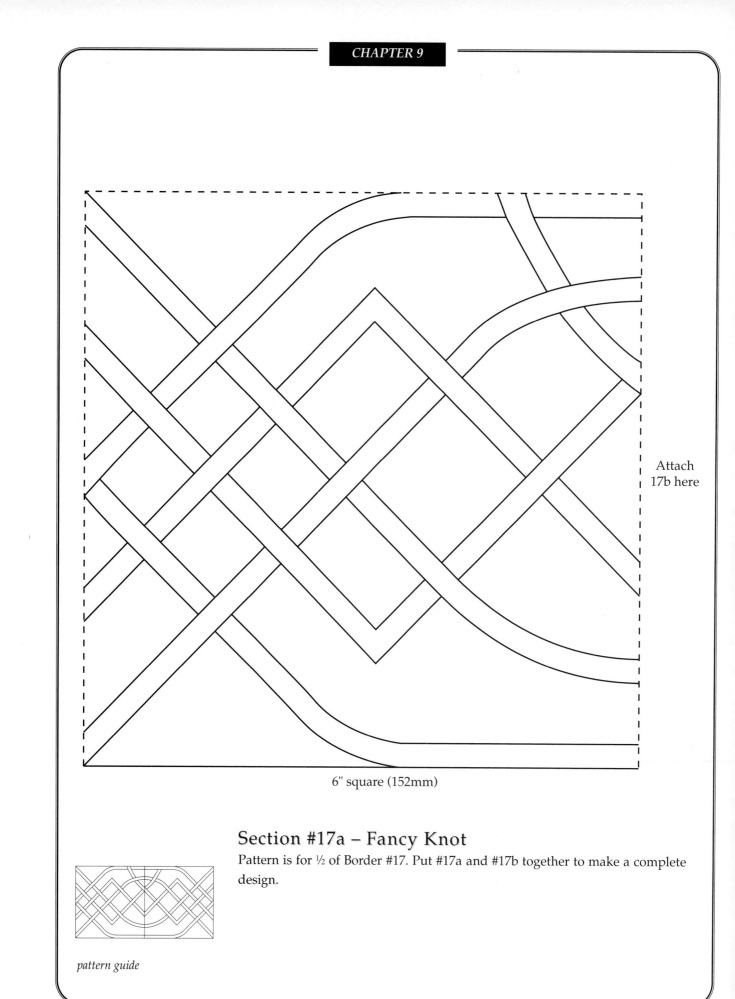

Attach
17b here

6" square (152mm)

Section #17a – Fancy Knot

Pattern is for ½ of Border #17. Put #17a and #17b together to make a complete design.

pattern guide

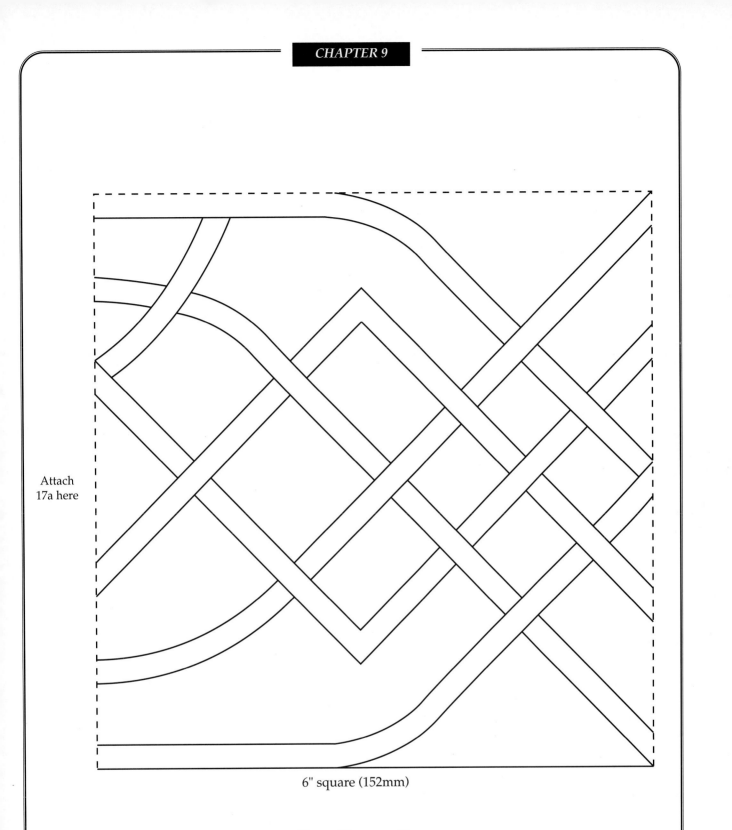

Attach
17a here

6" square (152mm)

Section #17b – Fancy Knot

Pattern is for ½ of Border #17. Put #17a and #17b together to make a complete design.

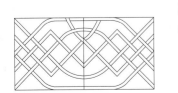

pattern guide

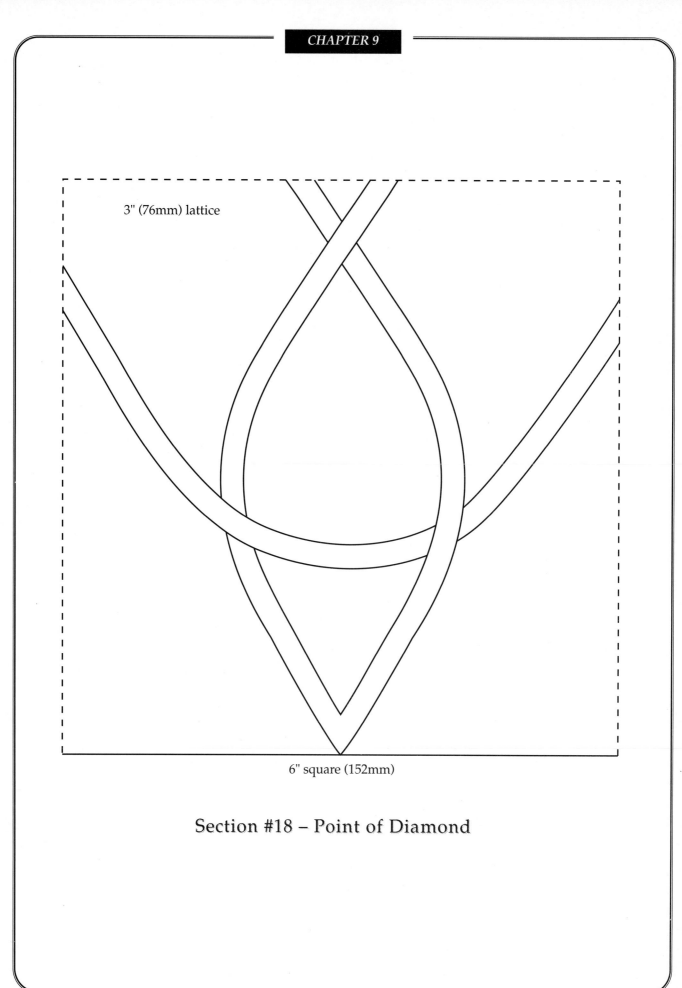

3" (76mm) lattice

6" square (152mm)

Section #18 – Point of Diamond

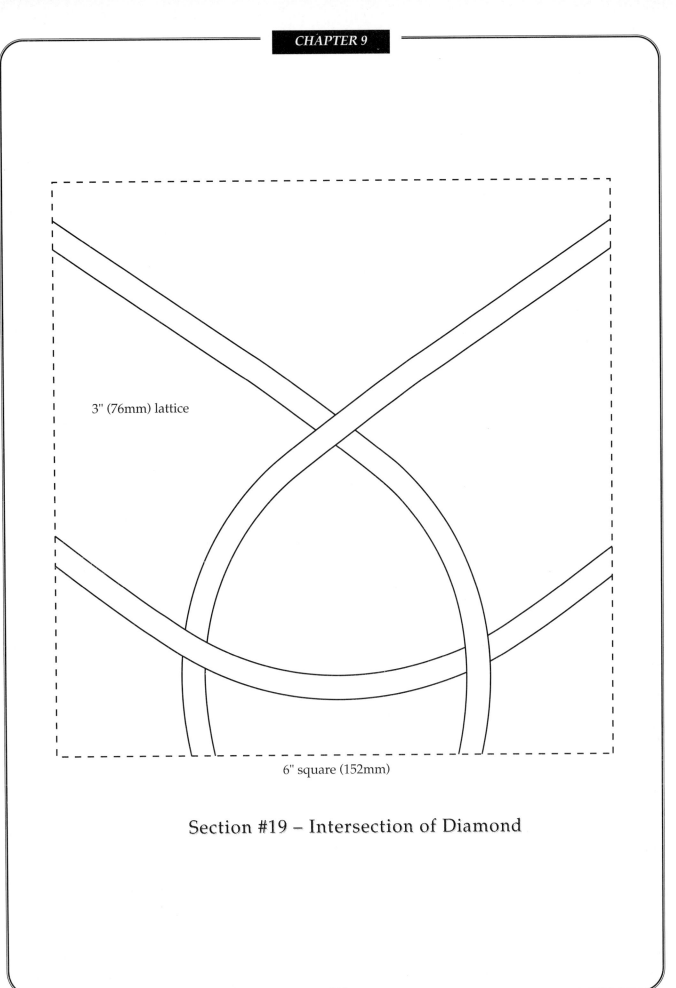

3" (76mm) lattice

6" square (152mm)

Section #19 – Intersection of Diamond

6" square (152mm)

Section #20 – Swirl Corner

Match to 21b

6" x 7¼" (152mm x 184mm)

Section #21a – Side Knot

pattern guide

Match to 21a

6" x 7¼" (152mm x 184mm)

Section #21b – Side Knot

pattern guide

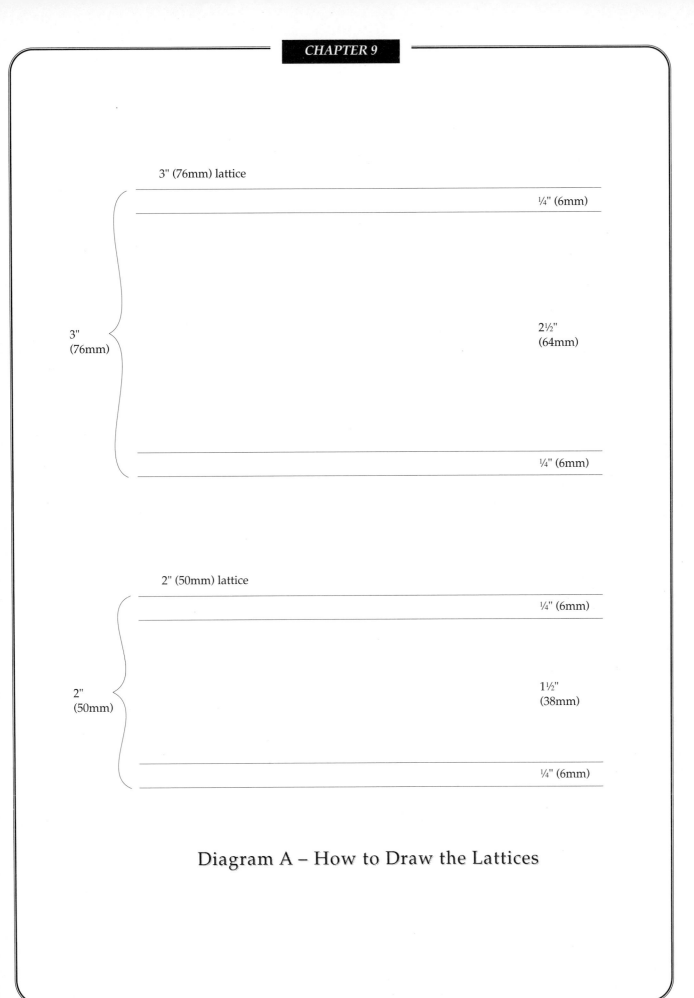

3" (76mm) lattice

¼" (6mm)

3"
(76mm)

2½"
(64mm)

¼" (6mm)

2" (50mm) lattice

¼" (6mm)

2"
(50mm)

1½"
(38mm)

¼" (6mm)

Diagram A – How to Draw the Lattices

BIBLIOGRAPHY

Bain, George. *Celtic Art: The Methods of Construction.* New York, New York: Dover Publications, 1973.

Bain, Iain. *Celtic Knotwork.* New York, New York: Sterling Publishing Co., 1992.

Dietrich, Mimi. *Happy Endings.* Bothell, Washington: That Patchwork Place, 1988.

Fons, Marianne. *Fine Feathers.* Lafayette, California: C&T Publishing, 1988.

Hargrave, Harriet. *Heirloom Machine Quilting, Revised.* Lafayette, California: C&T Publishing, 1990.

Marston, Gwen and Joe Cunningham. *Quilting with Style.* Paducah, Kentucky: American Quilter's Society, 1993.

McKelvey, Susan Richardson. *Color for Quilters.* Atlanta, Georgia: Yours Truly, 1984.

Penders, Mary Coyne. *Color and Cloth.* San Francisco, California: Quilt Digest Press, 1989.

Seidensticker, Edward G., translator and abridger. *The Tale of Genji* (source of quotation used in the dedication). New York, New York: Random House, 1985.

Sienkiewitcz, Elly. *Appliqué 12 Easy Ways!* Lafayette, California: C&T Publishing, 1991.

Wiechec, Philomena. *Celtic Quilt Designs.* Sunnyvale, California: Celtic Design Co., 1980.

SOURCES FOR SUPPLIES

APPLIQUÉ NEEDLES AND NEEDLE THREADERS:

Keepsake Quilting
Route 25
P.O. Box 1618
Centre Harbor, NH 03226-1618

FASTUBE™ FOOT:

The Crowning Touch
2410 Glory C Road
Medford, OR 97504

MARBLED FABRIC BY MARJORIE LEE BEVIS:

Marbled Fabric & Accessories
325 4th St.
Petaluma, CA 94952

METAL BIAS BARS:

Celtic Design Co.
P.O. Box 2643
Sunnyvale, CA 94087-0643

TOPSTITCHING OR EDGESTITCHING FOOT:

Nancy's Notions, Ltd.
P.O. Box 683
Beaver Dam, WI 53916-0683

American Quilter's Society

dedicated to publishing books for today's quilters

The following AQS publications are currently available:

- **Adapting Architectural Details for Quilts,** Carol Wagner, #2282: AQS, 1991, 88 pages, softbound, $12.95
- **American Beauties: Rose & Tulip Quilts,** Gwen Marston & Joe Cunningham, #1907: AQS, 1988, 96 pages, softbound, $14.95
- **Appliqué Designs: My Mother Taught Me to Sew,** Faye Anderson, #2121: AQS, 1990, 80 pages, softbound, $12.95
- **Appliqué Patterns from Native American Beadwork Designs,** Dr. Joyce Mori, #3790: AQS, 1994, 96 pages, softbound, $14.95
- **Arkansas Quilts: Arkansas Warmth,** Arkansas Quilter's Guild, Inc., #1908: AQS, 1987, 144 pages, hardbound, $24.95
- **The Art of Hand Appliqué,** Laura Lee Fritz, #2122: AQS, 1990, 80 pages, softbound, $14.95
- **...Ask Helen More About Quilting Designs,** Helen Squire, #2099: AQS, 1990, 54 pages, 17 x 11, spiral-bound, $14.95
- **Award-Winning Quilts & Their Makers, Vol. I: The Best of AQS Shows – 1985-1987,** #2207: AQS, 1991, 232 pages, softbound, $24.95
- **Award-Winning Quilts & Their Makers, Vol. II: The Best of AQS Shows – 1988-1989,** #2354: AQS, 1992, 176 pages, softbound, $24.95
- **Award-Winning Quilts & Their Makers, Vol. III: The Best of AQS Shows – 1990-1991,** #3425: AQS, 1993, 180 pages, softbound, $24.95
- **Award-Winning Quilts & Their Makers, Vol. IV: The Best of AQS Shows – 1992-1993,** #3791: AQS, 1994, 180 pages, softbound, $24.95
- **Classic Basket Quilts,** Elizabeth Porter & Marianne Fons, #2208: AQS, 1991, 128 pages, softbound, $16.95
- **A Collection of Favorite Quilts,** Judy Florence, #2119: AQS, 1990, 136 pages, softbound, $18.95
- **Creative Machine Art,** Sharee Dawn Roberts, #2355: AQS, 1992, 142 pages, 9 x 9, softbound, $24.95
- **Dear Helen, Can You Tell Me?...All about Quilting Designs,** Helen Squire, #1820: AQS, 1987, 51 pages, 17 x 11, spiral-bound, $12.95
- **Double Wedding Ring Quilts: New Quilts from an Old Favorite,** #3870: AQS, 1994, 112 pages, softbound, $14.95
- **Dye Painting!,** Ann Johnston, #3399: AQS, 1992, 88 pages, softbound, $19.95
- **Dyeing & Overdyeing of Cotton Fabrics,** Judy Mercer Tescher, #2030: AQS, 1990, 54 pages, softbound, $9.95
- **Encyclopedia of Pieced Quilt Patterns,** compiled by Barbara Brackman, #3468: AQS, 1993, 552 pages, hardbound, $34.95
- **Flavor Quilts for Kids to Make: Complete Instructions for Teaching Children to Dye, Decorate & Sew Quilts,** Jennifer Amor, #2356: AQS, 1991, 120 pages, softbound, $12.95
- **From Basics to Binding: A Complete Guide to Making Quilts,** Karen Kay Buckley, #2381: AQS, 1992, 160 pages, softbound, $16.95
- **Fun & Fancy Machine Quiltmaking,** Lois Smith, #1982: AQS, 1989, 144 pages, softbound, $19.95
- **The Grand Finale: A Quilter's Guide to Finishing Projects,** Linda Denner, #1924: AQS, 1988, 96 pages, softbound, $14.95
- **Heirloom Miniatures,** Tina M. Gravatt, #2097: AQS, 1990, 64 pages, softbound, $9.95
- **Infinite Stars,** Gayle Bong, #2283: AQS, 1992, 72 pages, softbound, $12.95
- **The Ins and Outs: Perfecting the Quilting Stitch,** Patricia J. Morris, #2120: AQS, 1990, 96 pages, softbound, $9.95
- **Irish Chain Quilts: A Workbook of Irish Chains & Related Patterns,** Joyce B. Peaden, #1906: AQS, 1988, 96 pages, softbound, $14.95
- **Jacobean Appliqué: Book I, "Exotica,"** Patricia B. Campbell & Mimi Ayars, Ph.D, #3784: AQS, 1993, 160 pages, softbound, $18.95
- **The Judge's Task: How Award-Winning Quilts Are Selected,** Patricia J. Morris, #3904: AQS, 1993, 128 pages, softbound, $19.95
- **The Log Cabin Returns to Kentucky: Quilts from the Pilgrim/Roy Collection,** Gerald Roy and Paul Pilgrim, #3329: AQS, 1992, 36 pages, 9 x 7, softbound, $12.95
- **Marbling Fabrics for Quilts: A Guide for Learning & Teaching,** Kathy Fawcett & Carol Shoaf, #2206: AQS, 1991, 72 pages, softbound, $12.95
- **More Projects and Patterns: A Second Collection of Favorite Quilts,** Judy Florence, #3330: AQS, 1992, 152 pages, softbound, $18.95
- **Nancy Crow: Quilts and Influences,** Nancy Crow, #1981: AQS, 1990, 256 pages, 9 x 12, hardcover, $29.95
- **Nancy Crow: Work in Transition,** Nancy Crow, #3331: AQS, 1992, 32 pages, 9 x 10, softbound, $12.95
- **New Jersey Quilts – 1777 to 1950: Contributions to an American Tradition,** The Heritage Quilt Project of New Jersey; text by Rachel Cochran, Rita Erickson, Natalie Hart & Barbara Schaffer, #3332: AQS, 1992, 256 pages, softbound, $29.95
- **No Dragons on My Quilt,** Jean Ray Laury with Ritva Laury & Lizabeth Laury, #2153: AQS, 1990, 52 pages, hardcover, $12.95
- **Oklahoma Heritage Quilts,** Oklahoma Quilt Heritage Project #2032: AQS, 1990, 144 pages, softbound, $19.95
- **Old Favorites in Miniature,** Tina Gravatt #3469: AQS, 1993, 104 pages, softbound, $15.95
- **A Patchwork of Pieces: An Anthology of Early Quilt Stories 1845-1940,** complied by Cuesta Ray Benberry and Carol Pinney Crabb, #3333: AQS, 1993, 360 pages, 5½ x 8½, softbound, $14.95
- **Quilt Groups Today: Who They Are, Where They Meet, What They Do, and How to Contact Them – A Complete Guide for 1992-1993,** #3308: AQS, 1992, 336 pages, softbound, $14.95
- **Quilt Registry,** Lynne Fritz, #2380: AQS, 1992, 80 pages, hardbound, $9.95
- **Quilting Patterns from Native American Designs,** Dr. Joyce Mori, #3467: AQS, 1993, 80 pages, softbound, $12.95
- **Quilting with Style: Principles for Great Pattern Design,** Gwen Marston & Joe Cunningham, #3470: AQS, 1993, 192 pages, 9 x 12, hardbound, $24.95
- **Quiltmaker's Guide: Basics & Beyond,** Carol Doak, #2284: AQS, 1992, 208 pages, softbound, $19.95
- **Quilts: Old & New, A Similar View,** Paul D. Pilgrim and Gerald R. Roy, #3715: AQS, 1993, 40 pages, softbound, $12.95
- **Quilts: The Permanent Collection – MAQS,** #2257: AQS, 1991, 100 pages, 10 x 6½, softbound, $9.95
- **Seasons of the Heart & Home: Quilts for a Winter's Day,** Jan Patek, #3796: AQS, 1993, 160 pages, softbound, $18.95
- **Seasons of the Heart & Home: Quilts for Summer Days,** Jan Patek, #3761: AQS, 1993, 160 pages, softbound, $18.95
- **Sensational Scrap Quilts,** Darra Duffy Williamson, #2357: AQS, 1992, 152 pages, softbound, $24.95
- **Sets & Borders,** Gwen Marston & Joe Cunningham, #1821: AQS, 1987, 104 pages, softbound, $14.95
- **Show Me Helen...How to Use Quilting Designs,** Helen Squire, #3375: AQS, 1993, 155 pages, softbound, $15.95
- **Somewhere in Between: Quilts and Quilters of Illinois,** Rita Barrow Barber, #1790: AQS, 1986, 78 pages, softbound, $14.95
- **Spike & Zola: Patterns for Laughter...and Appliqué, Painting, or Stenciling,** Donna French Collins, #3794: AQS, 1993, 72 pages, softbound, $9.95
- **Stenciled Quilts for Christmas,** Marie Monteith Sturmer, #2098: AQS, 1990, 104 pages, softbound, $14.95
- **Three-Dimensional Appliqué and Embroidery Embellishment: Techniques for Today's Album Quilt,** Anita Shackelford, #3788: AQS, 1993, 152 pages, 9 x 12, hardbound, $24.95
- **A Treasury of Quilting Designs,** Linda Goodmon Emery, #2029: AQS, 1990, 80 pages, 14 x 11, spiral-bound, $14.95
- **Tricks with Chintz: Using Large Prints to Add New Magic to Traditional Quilt Blocks,** Nancy S. Breland, #3847: AQS, 1994, 96 pages, softbound, $14.95
- **Wonderful Wearables: A Celebration of Creative Clothing,** Virginia Avery, #2286: AQS, 1991, 184 pages, softbound, $24.95

These books can be found in local bookstores and quilt shops. If you are unable to locate a title in your area, you can order by mail from AQS, P.O. Box 3290, Paducah, KY 42002-3290. Please add $1 for the first book and 40¢ for each additional one to cover postage and handling. (International orders please add $1.50 for the first book and $1 for each additional one.)